Saffron
and profit

Content

WARNING:

WHILE I DO NOT BELIEVE THAT ONE SHOULD CULTIVATE SOLELY FOR FINANCIAL GAIN, AND BEING A FAN OF BILL AND HIS FRIENDS, I OFFER YOU SEVERAL TOOLS TO THOROUGHLY AND TECHNICALLY UNDERSTAND, AND PERHAPS EVEN TOO MUCH, EVERYTHING YOU NEED TO KNOW ABOUT SAFFRON BEFORE EVEN CONSIDERING SELLING IT.

IT IS UP TO YOU TO MAKE GOOD USE OF THEM...

The origin, history, and legends.

Saffron is a precious and ancient spice with historical references dating back to ancient times. The first historical mentions of saffron can be traced back to sacred scriptures, where it was referred to as "Karkum." Later, the plant's name "Crocus" is attributed to the Greek term "Kroke," meaning "thread of fabric," in reference to the plant's filamentous stigmas used for commercial purposes.

In the ancient civilizations of the Mediterranean, saffron is remembered in various forms, from pictorial depictions in Knossos to references in the Egyptian Ebers Papyrus (1500 BCE) and the Song of Songs in the Old Testament (IV, 14).

As is often the case in the classical world, mythology has also constructed stories related to botany. For saffron, also known as "crocus," there are two mythological stories: in the first, Mercury's companion named Crocus is fatally wounded by a poorly thrown discus, and from the earth soaked with his blood, the yellow and red plant emerges. In the second version, the nymph Smila falls in love with Crocus and, as punishment, Diana transforms him into a saffron plant.

The exact geographical origin of saffron is not entirely certain, but many scholars place it in the region between Crete and the Middle East. From there, it rapidly spread to India and China, and later, thanks to the Arabs, to the Mediterranean area. The precise origin seems to be associated with Greece, Asia Minor, and Persia. Saffron cultivation began in the late Bronze Age and was extensively grown in the East and the Mediterranean basin.

The cultivation of saffron in India, particularly in Kashmir, has a documented history dating back to 550 AD. Experts believe that saffron initially spread to India through the efforts of Persian rulers who sought to supply their gardens and parks with new plants by transplanting cultivars throughout the Persian Empire.

Another variation of the theory about the introduction of saffron in Kashmir suggests that after ancient Persia conquered Kashmir, Persian saffron bulbs were planted in the region. The first harvest occurred around 500 BC. Therefore, the saffron growing in Kashmir originated from Persia. It is said that saffron was cultivated in Padampore (now called Pampore), a location about 13 km from Srinagar in Kashmir, India. The cultivation also spread to other alluvial plains such as Budgam, Tsrar, and the southern part of Kashmir.

In Italy, the introduction of saffron is believed to be attributed to a monk who was part of the Inquisition Tribunal, and he brought the first saffron bulbs to his homeland in the province of L'Aquila. However, there are writings that attest to saffron cultivation in Sicily during the Greco-Roman era, with Centuripe saffron (Crocus Centuripunus) being particularly renowned. In Centuripe, saffron cultivation was encouraged, and the high-quality product was suitable for perfumes and was exported to Pozzuoli. This activity required the labor of many workers to collect the ephemeral stigmas of the flower in the morning or evening, which were then dried (5 kilograms of fresh stigmas to obtain one kilogram of dried saffron).

The word "saffron" originates from the French "safran," which, in turn, comes from the Latin "safranum." "Safranum" also refers to the Italian "zafferano" and the Spanish "azafrán." This word derives from the Arabic "asfar," meaning "yellow," through the anonymous "zafran," the name of the spice in Arabic.

Almost all European languages and several non-European languages have borrowed the name of saffron. "Crocus" comes from the Greek word "Corycus," which is the name of an area in the Cilicia region in the eastern Mediterranean. The scientific name "Crocus" derives from the Greek term "Krokòs," which, in turn, originates from the Hebrew "Karkòm," derived from the Phoenician word "Cartamus." This term refers to a plant species believed to impart a yellow color.

The virtues of saffron have been known since ancient times, and it is not surprising that it was widely used in the preparation of remedies against the plague. The Egyptians were familiar with its therapeutic properties, as mentioned in the Ebers Papyrus. The oldest graphic representation of saffron dates back to 1400 BC and is preserved in the Heraklion Museum on the island of Crete. It is a mural painting from ancient Knossos.

Hippocrates, the renowned physician of ancient Greece, prescribed saffron in poultices to alleviate the pain of gout and rheumatism. These therapeutic properties have also been confirmed in more recent times.

Around 1370, Guillaume Tirel, known as Taillevent, the first head chef of Charles VI, King of France, included saffron among the essential aromas to always be present in the kitchen, as recorded in his cookbook called "Viandier." During that period, saffron was likely still an imported product. Interestingly, many centuries earlier, in 882, the "Capitularies of Villis" of Charlemagne, which regulated the activities of estates, did not include saffron among the over one hundred plants that the lord of the estate had to cultivate for the availability of the castle and the village.

Even in 1549, Cristoforo da Messisburgo, the steward at the court of Cardinal Ippolito d'Este in Ferrara and author of the fundamental text "Banchetti e composizione di vivande" (Banquets and the Composition of Foods), mentions the "croco" (probably referring to saffron pistils) as one of the dried spices, but not among cultivated products. This indicates the importance of the irreplaceable aroma of saffron even a century after the descriptions in other sources. Platine, in the famous humanistic cookbook "Della onesta voluttà" (On Honest Pleasure), states that saffron enhances dishes that require improvement in color and flavor.

At the Este court in Ferrara, saffron was exalted in various recipes, such as "rice in broth with egg yolks and saffron," known as "alla siciliana." This suggests that saffron was widely used to add color and exquisite flavor to dishes.

According to Pliny the Elder, saffron had a wide range of therapeutic uses, helping to alleviate ulcers in the stomach, chest, kidneys, liver, and lungs. It was considered useful for coughs and chest pain, and interestingly, it was believed to be an aphrodisiac that could stimulate lust. Additionally, it was mainly imported from Cilicia because of its culinary and aphrodisiac properties.

Apicius, the renowned Roman gastronome, mentions saffron as an ingredient in Roman absinthe wine, giving the wine a digestive touch.

Pliny and Aulus Celsus report that saffron was the main component of a special eye lotion called "diaciocu," which was particularly effective.

In the Salerno School of Medicine, saffron is described as an agent that comforts, soothes, and strengthens the limbs and liver, possessing healing properties.

During the Middle Ages, saffron was considered a bringer of joy, so much so that a cheerful person was said to have "slept on a sack of saffron." The preciousness of this spice led to specific regulations and laws governing its trade, and the maritime Republics established "Saffron Banks" to manage its commerce and importation.

Dioscorides regarded saffron as an effective antispasmodic and anticonvulsant, while other scholars like Hippocrates, Theophrastus, and Galen attributed medicinal and indulgent properties to saffron. The Arabs also considered it useful as an emmenagogue, stimulating the menstrual flow.

In the "Materia Medica" by Pedanius Dioscorides, the therapeutic effects of saffron known in antiquity are listed. In the translation of this work, carried out by the Sienese botanical physician Matthioli in his book on Dioscorides, the following passages can be read:

"Some say that crocus, taken with water in a quantity of three drams, produces a great feeling of joy. It has the virtue of ripening, softening, and slightly constricting; it stimulates urination and imparts a radiant appearance. When taken with sweet wine, it helps against drunkenness. Applied with breast milk, it stops the flow of the eyes; added to beverages, it soothes intestinal pains. Used as poultices, saffron bandages are beneficial for alleviating menstrual pains or applied on wounds and inflammations. Furthermore, it stimulates lust. Even Homer speaks of it as a fragrance and medicine."

During the Renaissance era, saffron was considered a calming remedy for coughs, an aid for metabolism improvement, and even used as an abortifacient in medicinal properties. It was also believed to have digestive benefits as a food ingredient.

Saffron was present in almost all recipes, to the extent that it led to the belief that every remedy against the plague had a yellow color, establishing a connection between the color of the remedy and that of the afflicted person in the treatment of the disease. According to the principle of "similitudes" cherished by Paracelsus and his school, this connection might make sense, as the physician Giovanni De Albertis in the 15th century added a note based on his personal experience, observing that plague patients had an "almost jaundiced" complexion.

Pliny recalls the use of an ointment called "crocromagna,"

which was used for cataracts. This ointment was translated as "saffron dregs" and was also employed in medical applications. It is believed that crocromagna was the residue left after saffron oil extraction.

Saffron was an important ingredient in various antipestilential medicinal preparations, such as the "pillole di Ruso" or "pillole di Tribus," considered "ancient," as well as in scented preservative sachets and diaphoretics that were used to eliminate plague toxins through sweating. Saffron was also used in recipes like Teriaca, Mitridate, Hiera by Galen, Elixir Vitae, and masterful plague-fighting pills, as well as in blister plasters and liniments applied to the body to promote the maturation of buboes.

Even today, saffron is used as a stomachic or coloring agent, but it can also have stimulating or depressive effects on the nervous system, leading to hypnotic states. This recalls an ancient medical saying: "saffron oil inhaled through the nostrils induces sleep." Its use in medicine has ancient roots, and it has been considered a versatile and valuable remedy over the centuries.

Saffron contains an essential oil composed mainly of safranal. A common recognition test is to add a drop of sulfuric acid to saffron powder, which changes the color from blue to purple.

In the market, saffron is distinctly classified based on its origin: Italian saffron, with the one from L'Aquila being the most prized; French or Gatinois saffron, also highly esteemed; Spanish saffron, which is sometimes adulterated to improve its appearance; and Eastern saffron, considered of inferior quality.

To adulterate saffron, some species used were safflower and turmeric, which were also used by painters as dyes. The autumn crocus, a plant from the Lily family, was known as "wild saffron" and used for its beneficial external properties against gout. Some sophisticated substances from that period included the "aperitif crocus of Mars," a preparation of ferric carbonate and hydrated ferric oxide, and "antimony saffron," a brown antimony oxide.

Saffron was used both as a drug and as a dye to color fabrics yellow. Although it was known since ancient times and cultivated in Italy, its production suffered a decline during the barbaric period, limited to monastery gardens. However, from the 11th century, saffron cultivation began to rise again, and its commercialization was documented in Italian cities and throughout the Mediterranean.

In Tuscany, especially in the surroundings of Siena, San Gimignano, and Volterra, saffron was cultivated and then exported in large quantities from the markets of San Gimignano through the maritime trade of Pisa to the markets of the Levant and North Africa. Genoese merchants traded both Tuscan saffron and that from France and Spain. The Venetians, on the other hand, were particularly involved in the trade of saffron from the Marche region and Abruzzo.

According to Petino, saffron production during the medieval period could reach up to 500 "some," equivalent to about 850 quintals. Italy, Spain, and France were the main producers, each accounting for almost one-third of the total production. Other minor producers included Austria, Hungary, and Moravia, while Turkey produced saffron of lower quality but at a lower price, thus providing competition.

In the decades around 1400, Tuscan saffron was considered the best, followed by Lombard saffron, which came close in terms of price. Saffron from L'Aquila would later match the quality of the first two, while saffron from the Marche region was of inferior quality. Other centers like Norcia, Spoleto, and Foligno offered saffron, but they did not reach the value of Tuscan saffron.

Indeed, saffron held significant economic importance during historical periods. One example illustrating its economic value is provided by the Florentine merchant Matteo Tinghi, who in 1376 bought saffron in Venice for 1000 florins and then resold it in Buda, thus doubling his invested capital.

Venice served as a major distribution center for Lombard, Tuscan, Marche, and Abruzzo saffron, exporting it to the Levant and selling it to German merchants. These German merchants were also present in Catalonia and eventually frequented the markets of Southern Italy. By the end of the 14th century, a colony of German merchants settled in L'Aquila. Florentine merchants were also active in the same city and traded saffron, as demonstrated by the business of the Della Casa-Guadagni family, which sold saffron in Geneva, imported from Santuccio dell'Aquila and Paolo di Sulmona. In 1480, a Florentine merchant, associated with the Strozzi family in Naples, purchased saffron in Tagliacozzo, Sulmona, Pettorano, Goriano, and Magliano, then sending it to Lombardy and the fairs in Lyon.

During the modern age, the exports of saffron from L'Aquila were primarily controlled by German merchants. Initially, exports amounted to 200 bales per year, approximately 180 quintals. However, starting from 1560, there was a significant increase that reached 300 quintals annually, with a value of 200,000 ducats. The German merchants continued to operate in L'Aquila, alongside the Florentines, who only departed in the late 1630s.

Nevertheless, in 1596, saffron exports began to decline, dropping to 150 quintals, and in the following years, it remained around 200 quintals until 1630. Subsequently, fiscal policies and the loss of the city's mercantile function led to the decline of saffron cultivation and trade. The economic activity linked to saffron at that time started losing its importance, marking the end of a prosperous era for L'Aquila as a productive and commercial center of this precious spice.

Economic importance

Statistics on saffron cultivation areas may vary due to the small size of the plots, often managed at the family level, which may escape official surveys in countries. As a result, the officially recorded areas may be lower than the actual ones present in the territory. Additionally, some producing countries consider saffron as a crop of secondary importance, and thus statistical data may not be available in certain regions, such as Austria, Libya, and Mexico.

Among the main saffron-producing countries, Iran stands out as the leading producer with an extensive cultivation area of approximately 47,000 hectares and a production of around 160 tons. India contributes to the production with approximately 2,500 hectares cultivated mainly in the states of Kashmir and Jammu, producing 8 to 10 tons of saffron.

In Europe, the main saffron-producing provinces include Castilla-La Mancha in Spain, with approximately 200 hectares cultivated and an annual production of 300-500 kg of saffron. Western Macedonia in Greece is another significant region, with around 860 hectares cultivated and an annual production of approximately 4,000-6,000 kg, much of which is exported to various countries such as Germany, Switzerland, China, Sweden, the United Kingdom, and the USA, as well as to a lesser extent to Italy and Spain.

Other countries, such as Turkey, Algeria, Egypt, France, Germany, Russia, Switzerland, and others, cultivate saffron on smaller areas, contributing overall to the global production of this precious spice.

In Italy, saffron cultivation covers about 8 hectares in Abruzzo, in the Navelli plain, and other small cultivated areas can be found in Tuscany, Calabria, and Sicily, bringing the total to approximately 35 hectares across the country. The main importing countries of saffron include Germany, Italy, the USA, Switzerland, France, and the United Kingdom, while the major exporting countries are Iran, Greece, Morocco, Azerbaijan, and Spain.

In 2004, the European Union produced approximately 6,800 kg of saffron, accounting for about 4% of the estimated world production of 170 tons. However, the cultivated area has decreased over time due to the high demand for labor and the increase in the standard of living in Mediterranean saffron-producing countries.

Chemical composition

Saffron contains over 150 volatile components that give it its characteristic aroma. Among its main constituents are carotenoids, including crocetin and its glycosidic derivatives such as crocin. Other carotenoids present are α-carotene, β-carotene, lycopene, and zeaxanthin.

The glycosidic forms of crocetin include digentiobioside (crocins), gentiobioside, glucoside, gentioglucoside, and diglucoside. Crocin is the most abundant component, also known for its presence in the fruit of Gardenia jasminoides. Other important components of saffron include picrocrocin, responsible for its bitter taste, and its related compound safranal, which contributes to its aroma.

The scent, taste, and pigments of saffron are primarily found in the red stigmatic lobes of the flower. In addition to carotenoids, saffron also contains anthocyanins, flavonoids, vitamins, amino acids, proteins, starch, mineral substances, gums, and other chemical residues.

Dried saffron stigmas contain about 10-12% water, 5-7% mineral matter, 5-8% fat, 12-13% protein, 20% reduced sugars, 6-7% pentose, 9-10% gums and dextrins, and a small amount of free sugars. The essential oil present in saffron is approximately 0.3%. Crocin and other components give saffron its unique aromatic, color, and flavor properties, making it a valuable and versatile spice in both cuisine and traditional medicine.

Several minor components belonging to different classes of natural substances have been isolated from the stigmas and other parts of the saffron plant. Terpenoids are the most common compounds found, including crocusatins present in the stigmas and petals, known for their significant antityrosinase activity.

Some glycosidic derivatives belonging to the class of terpenoids are considered precursors of the volatile components of saffron, offering alternatives to picrocrocin concerning its bitter taste.

In addition to terpenoids, several flavonoids have recently been highlighted in saffron stigmas. These polyphenols, together with picrocrocin, may contribute to the characteristic bitter taste of saffron.

The action plan of secondary metabolites in Crocus sativus also includes some anthraquinones isolated from the corms and an anthocyanin isolated from the petals, adding further components to the complexity of saffron's chemical composition.

Properties and Uses

Saffron is a precious spice with therapeutic, seasoning, and coloring properties. It is widely used in the food, dairy, and dye industries, as well as in cooking, medicine, cosmetics, perfumery, and flavored tobacco. Culinary traditions of various cultures, such as Arabic, Asian, European, and Indian, harness the characteristic honey-like aroma and herbal notes of saffron, adding a unique flavor to their dishes. Moreover, saffron imparts a vibrant yellow-orange hue to the dishes it is used in.

The main active substances in saffron include picrocrocin, safranal, and crocin. Picrocrocin provides its distinctive bittering power and, during drying and storage, breaks down into glucose and safranal, responsible for the distinctive aroma. Crocin, derived from crocetin, belongs to the family of natural colorants called carotenoids and imparts the beautiful yellow-orange color of saffron.

These active substances in saffron exert specific and relevant properties, but due to the small quantities generally used in cooking, it is not always possible to fully obtain their therapeutic benefits.

Saffron contains small amounts of vitamins, including beta-carotene (provitamin A), thiamine (vitamin B1), and riboflavin (vitamin B2). The active compounds present in saffron confer various pharmacological properties to the product, including sedative, expectorant, eupeptic, gum analgesic, and gastric motility-stimulating effects. However, at high doses, it can have abortive effects.

A documented case involves a woman who ingested a high amount of saffron (5 grams dissolved in milk), leading to severe blood coagulation issues and severe histological damage.

Some of the active compounds in saffron have demonstrated beneficial effects in various situations: for example, crocetin increases blood oxygenation in vitro and in vivo and may be useful in the treatment of emphysema and cardiovascular diseases. Crocin, found in saffron, has shown effectiveness in treating painful dysmenorrhea and has demonstrated antibacterial activity against certain microorganisms.

However, it is important to emphasize that the use of saffron for therapeutic purposes should be done with caution and under the supervision of a medical professional, as high doses may cause unwanted and health-related issues.

Safranal, one of the active compounds in saffron, has proven effective in treating chronic bronchitis since it is eliminated through the lungs, exerting an anesthetic effect on the nerve endings of bronchial alveoli, thereby helping to alleviate coughing.

Despite the significant therapeutic properties of saffron's active compounds, obtaining these benefits may be challenging due to their small quantities in the spice.

However, saffron remains an extraordinary and irreplaceable food additive thanks to its aromatic and coloring properties. In the past, the confectionery industry used saffron to give products a uniform color, avoiding excessive use of eggs to achieve the same result. This was particularly important in ensuring a consistent and homogeneous production of sweets such as panettone, sponge cake, and biscuits.

The use of a non-toxic, natural colorant with a pleasant aroma, such as saffron, was widely accepted and adopted by all confectionery industries. This contributed to improving the quality of products and satisfying consumers' tastes.

Today, considering the wide range of sweets and beverages available in the market, promoting the use of saffron as a natural colorant in the food, confectionery, and liquor industries, instead of chemical dyes, could revitalize saffron cultivation, encouraging its growth and production.

The main destinations for saffron are, in order: the liquor industry, the food industry for domestic use, and the pharmaceutical industry. The latter seems to be expanding, with a return to the use of saffron as a medicinal substance, utilizing ancient Galenic preparations.

The liquor industry

Saffron finds its main application in the liquor industry, where it is used in the preparation of alcoholic aperitifs such as bitters, vermouth, and fernet, as well as in sweets and confectionery. Its coloring and flavoring properties are provided by active components such as crocin, crocetin, picrocrocin, safranal, and other volatile principles responsible for its characteristic "bouquet."

In liquor preparations, each product can choose to emphasize certain of these components, adjusting solubility, temperature, and contact times. In the past, saffron was also used in perfumery, but this practice seems to be no longer in use.

Today, it is common to introduce saffron in the preparation of rum, appreciating its alcoholic strength and aromatic properties.

The food industry

Saffron is widely used as a seasoning in the preparation of traditional dishes in some areas of the country, such as arancini and risotto alla milanese. Abroad, many traditional dishes, such as paella valenciana, meat and vegetable couscous, and bouillabaisse, include saffron as an essential ingredient, as it provides strong coloring power, a distinctive aroma, and a unique flavor.

To ensure consistent organoleptic characteristics, the Italian food industry creates blends of saffron from different sources. Each type of saffron can have different coloring power and aroma depending on its origin, preparation methods, and storage period.

In the past, saffron was also used as a coloring agent for pastes, butter, and cheeses. This practice, although neglected for a while, could experience a comeback as a genuine and natural coloring alternative to "artificial" colorants. Its use in food preparations is appreciated not only for the appearance and aroma it imparts to dishes but also for its contribution in making certain foods more digestible.

One gram of dried saffron has the capacity to color approximately 500 liters of water with an intense yellow tone. To add color to cheeses, it is sufficient to use 0.20 to 0.50 grams of saffron powder per 100 liters of milk.

The legend of the origin of "risotto alla milanese" tells of a painter who accidentally spilled the contents of a container of yellow dye (obtained with saffron) into the pot while cooking rice. Thanks to these characteristics, saffron is widely used in various baked goods, cheeses, pastry products, curries, liquors, meat dishes, and soups.

In various culinary cultures, such as in India, Iran, Spain, and other countries, saffron is used as a seasoning for rice. It is also a key ingredient in Indian milk-based sweets like gulab jamun, kulfi, double ka meetha, and in "saffron lassi," a popular spiced yogurt-based beverage in Jodhpur. Saffron imparts color and aroma to many Mediterranean and Middle Eastern dishes, especially rice, meat, fish, and Scandinavian and Balkan bread. Additionally, saffron is widely used in the perfume and dyeing industries.

Saffron has a wide range of uses in the culinary and textile worlds. It is often used to enhance the color, flavor, and aroma of various foods, such as ice creams, sauces, and dressings, giving them a golden hue and distinctive taste.

In the food industry, saffron serves as a coloring agent for sausages, butter, cheeses, puddings, pastries, rice curries, dairy products, and alcoholic and non-alcoholic beverages.

Another traditional use of saffron is as a coloring agent for honey, where saffron plants are placed near beehives to impart a more intense color and aroma to the honey, a practice already adopted by the Romans.

In the textile industry, saffron has been used to dye a wide range of materials, including veils, bandages, embroidery threads, sails, leather, glass, and ceramics. However, fixing the color in fabrics has been a challenge, and often a treatment with alum was necessary to achieve lasting results.

Today, due to its high cost, saffron is primarily used as an ingredient in food preparations to impart color and aroma to typical dishes. An example of this is the use of saffron in the production of "Piacentinu Ennese," a traditional cheese with ancient origins produced in the inland areas of Sicily. Saffron gives the cheese a distinctive aroma and color, contributing to its quality and unique characteristics.

The production and characteristics of "Piacentinu Ennese" mainly depend on the geographical environment in which it is produced, including the type of milk used, the rennet, and the production techniques. Human and natural factors play a significant role in influencing the cheese's characteristics.

Interessanti sono le diverse ipotesi riguardanti il nome "Piacentinu." Alcuni credono che il termine possa derivare da un riferimento al gusto piacevole e leggermente piccante del formaggio, attribuito alla presenza dello zafferano. Altri suggeriscono che il nome possa fare riferimento all'umidità che si forma all'interno del formaggio, dando l'idea della "lacrima" del formaggio. Esiste anche una teoria storica che collega il nome "Piacentinu" alla città di Piacenza, sebbene questa ipotesi sia meno popolare tra gli abitanti di Enna.

Inoltre, è interessante notare la leggenda che narra dell'origine del formaggio intorno al 1090, attribuita a Ruggero il Normanno. Secondo questa leggenda, preoccupato per la salute mentale di sua moglie che soffriva di una grave depressione ma amava molto i formaggi, Ruggero chiese ai casari di creare un formaggio dalle virtù taumaturgiche. Da qui nacque l'idea di aggiungere al caglio d'agnello una manciata di "Crocus sativus," una specie nota nell'antichità per le sue proprietà stimolanti ed energizzanti.

In addition to the legend, the "Piacentinu Ennese" has a documented history dating back to the 4th century AD. The historian Gallo, in a publication, mentions the use of saffron in the cheese, confirming the practice of adding this precious spice in the cheese production.

Among the irrefutable sources regarding the "Piacentinu Ennese," there is a manuscript written by Francesco Maja between 1681 and 1682, titled "Sicilia passeggiata," which provides details about the product. The ancient origin of the cheese, supported by the cited texts, confirms the interpretation given by the old producers to the term "piacentinu," which simply refers to the pleasantness of the product.

The "Piacentinu Ennese" is mainly obtained from the milk of Comisana sheep, to which saffron and black peppercorns are added to influence the taste and aroma. The cheese production still occurs using traditional techniques and ancient utensils. The milk with saffron coagulates in a wooden vat at a temperature of 32-35°C, using lamb or kid rennet paste for about 40-60 minutes. Subsequently, the curd is placed in reed baskets called "fascedde," which leave a particular molding on the surface of the cheese. During this process, black peppercorns are added. After that, the cheese is scalded, placed on wooden tables to dry, and then salted.

The day after production, the salting is carried out by hand on the entire surface of the cheese wheel. This operation is repeated at least twice at intervals of about 10 days, spreading on the cheese all the liquids expelled from the cheese during the process.

The "Piacentinu Ennese" cheese offers a unique taste, thanks to the presence of saffron, which is best appreciated in two different stages of maturation:

- In the semi-mature stage: the cheese is intended for table consumption and has an average maturation period ranging from 45 to 90 days, depending on the size of the wheel. In this phase, the cheese presents a slightly spicy taste and a distinctive saffron aroma.

- In the mature stage: the cheese is suitable both for table consumption and for grating. The maturation in this phase exceeds 90 days, giving the cheese a complexity of flavor and an intense saffron note.

Pharmacology

In recent times, there is a growing interest in the biological effects of saffron and its potential medical applications.

In the medical field, only the flower's stigmas and the upper part of the saffron style are used, as high doses (over 30 grams) can be toxic and abortive. However, saffron is attributed with various medicinal properties. In small doses, it acts as a gentle stimulant, while in larger doses, it can act as an aphrodisiac and narcotic. Since ancient times, saffron has been used in medicine to treat various human disorders, including cough, flatulence, colic, insomnia, chronic uterine bleeding, amenorrhea, smallpox, asthma, and cardiovascular disorders.

Indeed, saffron's properties go beyond traditional medicine, as some of its components show potential cytotoxic, anticarcinogenic, and antitumor effects. Saffron is used to alleviate depression and epilepsy gently. It has also been tested for gastric disorders and used as a pro-memory agent in rats. The anti-mutagenic, immunomodulatory, and antioxidant properties of saffron are well known.

Moreover, saffron is known for its anticonvulsant properties, making it an interesting subject of study for possible future medical applications.

In traditional Chinese medicine, saffron has long been used for its calming and blood-moving properties. It has been employed in the treatment of menstrual disorders and diseases related to high blood viscosity, including circulation problems. Its applications also extend to nervous disorders, helping to alleviate anxieties and hypnotic states, and supporting the treatment of central nervous system disorders.

The medical value of saffron was recorded in the book "YI-LIN-JI-YAO," a Chinese medical text from the 16th century, where the beneficial effects of "promoting blood circulation to eliminate impurities" were described. In the work "YINSHANZHENGYAO," dedicated to the importance of diet, there are 136 recipes that include saffron to treat various conditions.

Saffron has also played a significant role in traditional medicine in Azerbaijan and India, where it has been used to treat various diseases, including cancer, heart problems, eye disorders, blood-related conditions, and muscle paralysis. The long history of using this precious spice in different cultures testifies to its potential beneficial properties for human health.

Numerous pharmacological studies have highlighted the importance of saffron and its compounds. Miwa (1954) reported an inhibitory effect on the increase of bilirubin in the blood, while Gainer and Joines (1975) documented a decrease in cholesterol and triglyceride levels in the blood, thanks to the presence of crocin and crocetin. Several research studies have focused on the effects of saffron and its components on the central nervous system, revealing an interesting interaction with ethanol.

In another study, Zhang (1994) examined the effects of saffron extract on mice, demonstrating that a single oral administration of the extract reduced ethanol-induced memory impairment. The extract also reduced motor activity and prolonged the sleep time induced by hexobarbital. The author proposed four possible mechanisms of action:

1) Saffron facilitates alcohol detoxification, reducing its absorption in the gastrointestinal tract;

2) Saffron accelerates the elimination of alcohol from the brain, promoting its metabolism in the liver;

3) Saffron promotes blood circulation;

4) Saffron counteracts the pharmacological effects of ethanol on the central nervous system.

These findings indicate that saffron and its components may have a beneficial impact on health, including the ability to protect the nervous system and support liver function. These discoveries offer new perspectives for the potential use of saffron as a treatment or adjunct in certain medical conditions.

In another study conducted on anesthetized mice, it was observed that the long-term effect of saffron extract enhances stimulation in a specific area of the brain (Sugiura, 1995). This suggests that saffron acts as a long-lasting antagonist to ethanol, counteracting its effects at doses different from those that influence memory. The authors concluded that the results directly demonstrate the specific opposing action of saffron extract against ethanol, although the underlying mechanism for this effect has not been fully clarified yet.

Saffron and its components, particularly crocin, have been

the subject of numerous studies, showing that crocin appears to be an active antagonist to ethanol. These findings suggest that crocin might be responsible for the contrasting activity against ethanol and could play a key role in the beneficial effects of saffron on health.

Saffron and its components have demonstrated the ability to influence uterine tonicity, acting as regulators of uterine flow. However, in high doses, saffron can cause uterine bleeding and, therefore, lead to abortion. Conversely, studies have highlighted relaxing properties for the uterus, making it useful in the treatment of conditions such as dysmenorrhea and premenstrual syndrome (Leclerc, 1983).

Experiments conducted with various saffron extracts have shown stimulating actions on the uterus, both in pregnant and non-pregnant states, in guinea pigs, rabbits, and dogs. The underlying mechanism for these effects seems to involve both myogenic and neurogenic factors.

In addition, saffron extract has been indicated to possess antitumor activity, meaning it is capable of inhibiting the onset of cancer induced by carcinogenic agents. The first study to highlight the antitumor effect of saffron extract dates back to 1991. Oral administration of saffron extract in mice demonstrated effective inhibition of intraperitoneal tumor development of sarcoma-180, Erlich carcinoma, and Dalton's lymphoma. Mice with tumors treated with 200 mg of saffron extract per kg of body weight showed a significant extension of their lifespan, up to two or three times longer than untreated animals.

In a subsequent study, Nair (1994) highlighted that oral

administration of saffron extract in mice significantly inhibits the development of solid tumors derived from DLA and s-180 cells, but has no effect on EAC tumor cells. Furthermore, an increase in β-carotene and vitamin A levels in the serum of saffron-treated animals was observed, suggesting that this could be a possible antitumor mechanism.

Interesting results have also been obtained with the use of liposomes containing saffron extract injected into mice. An increase in the antitumor effect of this extract has been observed against various solid tumor cells, including EAC tumor cells, which were insensitive to oral administration of the extract. This increase in antitumor activity could be attributed to the direct delivery of the active substance or an increase in its solubility.

Studies on the use of saffron extract in combination with standard chemotherapy agents to reduce their toxicity have been particularly intriguing. This suggests a potential synergistic role between saffron and chemotherapy treatments, opening up new possibilities in the field of antitumor therapy.

Nair demonstrated that treatment with saffron extract prolongs the lifespan of mice compared to those treated with cisplatin alone, a well-known antitumor agent. Furthermore, saffron extract prevented the decrease in body weight, hemoglobin, and leukocyte count caused by cisplatin.

Similarly, Salomi reported that saffron extract increases the lifespan of mice treated with a lethal dose of cyclophosphamide.

Recently, it has been reported that crocetin, a component of saffron, increases the survival time and reduces tumor development (colon adenocarcinoma) in female mice, with no significant effect in male animals. The authors suggested that the selective antitumor action of crocetin in female mice is related to hormonal factors.

Crocetin, being a highly glycosylated carotenoid, is unusual in that it is water-soluble. Another carotenoid present in saffron is crocetin, characterized by a symmetrical diterpene structure with seven double bonds and four methyl groups.

Crocetin has been studied for its ability to increase the diffusivity of oxygen through liquids, such as plasma. This property allows crocetin to improve pulmonary oxygenation and alveolar oxygen transport. The efficacy of crocetin has been observed in the treatment of conditions such as cerebral hemorrhage, arthritis, and atherosclerosis.

Crocetin, present in saffron, shows remarkable ability to inhibit the development of skin tumors in mice exposed to benzoapyrene. Additionally, it has demonstrated inhibitory effects on intracellular nucleic acid alterations and protein synthesis in tumor cells. It has been noted to also act on the activity of protein kinase C and the proto-oncogene in INNIH13T3 cells.

These inhibitory effects of crocetin are most likely related to its potent antioxidant activity, which can counteract damages caused by free radicals.

Long-term studies on mice have shown that treatment with crocetin did not have harmful effects on the animals' metabolic alterations. However, a slight decrease in serum glucose levels was observed in mice treated with crocetin, but the underlying mechanism for this alteration is still unknown.

Some researchers suggest that an increase in insulin levels might be a possible cause, but further study is needed to fully understand this relationship. In any case, the potential benefits of crocetin in combating cancer and acting as an antioxidant seem to outweigh any mild side effects, and research continues to further explore its promising therapeutic properties.

Anti-tumor effects

Several hypotheses have been proposed to explain the anti-tumor and anti-carcinogenic effects of saffron and its constituents.

One of the proposed mechanisms involves the inhibitory effect on DNA and RNA synthesis within the cells. It is interesting to note that saffron extract has demonstrated the inhibition of RNA and DNA synthesis in malignant human cells, regardless of whether they transform into tumor cells or remain normal in vitro, but it did not show obvious inhibitory effects on non-malignant human cells.

A second mechanism of the anti-tumor action of saffron and its constituents involves the inhibitory effect on the free radical chain reaction. Since most carotenoids are liposoluble, they act as antioxidants, protecting cells from free radical damage.

A third hypothesized effect is the natural conversion of carotenoids into retinoids. However, recent studies have indicated that the conversion of carotenoids into vitamin A is not an essential requirement for anticancer activity.

A fourth mechanism of action involves the cytotoxic effect related to the interaction of carotenoids with the enzyme topoisomerase II, which is involved in the replication of cellular DNA. This theory is supported by the nuclear localization of some carotenoids and their inhibitory effect on cellular DNA synthesis. It has been hypothesized that saffron contains lecithin and that the anti-tumor activity of saffron may be mediated by this substance. The literature also contains reports of saffron extract and/or its components inhibiting the activity of various cellular enzymes, suggesting that the anti-tumor effect of these agents may be associated with their effect on enzymatic functions.

Treatment of tumor cells with saffron has shown an increase in intracellular levels of sulfide-containing compounds, which could contribute to explaining the cytotoxicity of saffron. Another suggested mechanism is that the cytotoxic effect of saffron carotenoids may be mediated by apoptosis, a process of programmed cell death.

Interesting studies have shown that encapsulating compounds extracted from saffron or saffron carotenoids in amorphous polymer matrices improves their stability and their anti-tumor effects. More recently, it has been observed that gamma radiation did not produce significant changes in the quality of saffron volatile oils but led to a reduction in glycosides and an increase in aglycones in saffron carotenoids. This relative stability of saffron to radiation should also be considered to explain its potential for chemoprevention.

In summary, research suggests that saffron may have various anti-tumor and chemopreventive properties, including the inhibition of enzymatic functions, the induction of apoptosis, and enhanced stability through encapsulation. However, further studies are needed to fully understand the underlying mechanisms and to assess its potential as a therapeutic agent in tumor prevention.

Botany

Saffron is an herbaceous plant belonging to the genus Crocus, species Crocus sativus L. It is characterized by perennial growth and reaches a height of 10 to 25 cm. The plant develops from corms, which are bulbous-tuberous formations commonly known as bulbs.

The saffron bulb is an underground stem flattened at the base, similar to an onion bulb. It consists of a compact mass of starch, resembling scaled leaves, covered by a tightly reticulated sheath called a tunic. From each newly formed bulb, 1 or 2 apical buds can develop, from which leaves and the floral axis originate, and 1 or 2 secondary buds, arranged irregularly in a spiral at the lower part of the bulb. The secondary buds give rise to a caudate axis and a cluster of leaves that utilize photosynthesis to obtain nutrients and grow.

The saffron seedlings develop adventitious roots that originate from the lower part of the bulb. There are three types of roots produced by saffron bulbs: absorbing roots (fibrous roots), contractile roots, and contractile-absorbing roots, each with specific structural characteristics and functions.

The fibrous roots are thin and numerous, emerging from a single ring at the base of the bulb. These roots are responsible for absorbing water and nutrients from the soil.

The contractile roots, also known as "drop roots" due to their shape, are large and whitish. They have the ability to contract and pull the bulb towards the ground, allowing the plant to position itself at the optimal depth for growth. Phenolic compounds, such as p-coumaric acid, play a positive role in the development and contraction of these roots.

Finally, there are the contractile-absorbing roots, which are thinner and longer than the contractile roots, and they develop near the shoots that host the contractile roots. These roots appear later compared to the contractile roots.

The saffron leaves are radical in shape, long and thin, resembling slender grass. They have a grooved surface, and the margins are curved and fringed. The color of the leaves is grayish-green with a slight whitish hue on the lower surface. The lower leaf is surrounded by sheaths of translucent and whitish tissue.

Saffron leaves can reach a length of about 50 cm and are very narrow, with a width ranging from 1.5 to 2.5 mm. The appearance of the leaves coincides with or immediately follows flowering. Each saffron bulb produces from 6 to 15 leaves.

The saffron flowers have an upright and regular shape. Each bulb produces from 1 to 3 flowers, with three purple sepals and three similar petals. The central pistil has a tubular ovary with a slender style. The style, brightly red in color, extends from the apex of the underground ovary through the perianth tube and divides into three filaments called stigmas.

Usually, there are one to three flowers per stem and up to 12 stems per plant. Flowering generally occurs in autumn, between September and November, simultaneously with the appearance of the leaves. Saffron flowers are characterized by a perianth consisting of a tube and a small funnel. The six segments of the perianth are under-lobed and divided into two series, with the inner ones slightly shorter than the outer ones, concave, and narrow. The tube throat is bearded.

In plants with bulbs that have formed flowering shoots, flowering can occur in two or three of the shoots closest to the bulb apex, while in bulbs with non-flowering shoots, the formation of the flower is usually limited to the apical and dominant shoot.

The androecium of saffron consists of three stamens, which are attached to the base of the outer segments, precisely at the throat of the perianth. The filaments of the stamens are short and free, while the anthers, yellow in color, are long and attached at the base.

The gynoecean, on the other hand, consists of the ovary, the style, and the stigmas. The style is thread-like and branches into three arms, known as stigmas, which protrude from the perianth. The stigmas are tubular, characterized by a reddish or orange-red color, and are swollen at the base. The stigmas constitute the precious commercial saffron, and their length varies from 2.0 to 3.2 cm. They form a narrower tube at the base, where they join the style, but extend towards the upper end, where they present a fissure on the inner side. A single saffron stigma weighs about 2 mg, and each flower has three stigmas. To produce 1 kg of saffron stigmas, as many as 150,000 flowers are needed.

The ovary is tricarpellary and has an oval shape, remaining hidden among the bases of the leaves. The capsule containing the seeds is fusiform, and the seeds themselves are round in shape.

It should be noted that saffron is a triploid species, which means it is sterile and reproduces only through vegetative methods.

The sterility of saffron is due to an irregular triploid meiosis process, characterized by many anomalies in sporogenic and gametophytic development, as well as excessive pollen production. About 70% of ovules in mature Crocus sativus plants contain a normal polyhedral sac, but a high incidence of low viability and pollen germination has been observed due to these meiotic anomalies. Therefore, saffron exhibits self-sterility, and in vitro cross-pollination with pollen from other Crocus species has yielded variable results.

Although some angiosperms can produce apodictic embryos, this situation has never been observed in saffron. The genetic origin of Crocus sativus is not yet fully clear, and there are several hypotheses regarding its possible ancestors.

Some theories suggest that saffron may have originated from an autotriploid of a wild Crocus, possibly through fertilization of a diploid egg cell that did not reduce correctly, or via an aploid egg cell with two aploid sperm. Another possibility is that saffron is an allopolyploid formed through the hybridization of Crocus cartwrightianus and Crocus hadriaticus.

Information about saffron's genealogy is not unanimous. A karyological study suggests that possible ancestors of Crocus sativus are Crocus cartwrightianus or Crocus thomasii. Further Amplified Fragment Length Polymorphism (AFLP) analysis has highlighted that the DNA characteristics of these ancestors are compatible with Crocus sativus, suggesting Crocus cartwrightianus as the most likely closest ancestor. Additionally, the flowering of Crocus cartwrightianus bears similarities to that of Crocus sativus. However, the exact origins of saffron require further research and investigation to be fully understood.

According to Bighton, saffron exhibits stable and uniform biological traits worldwide, differing only in minor morphological and biochemical characteristics, such as some morphometric features. A recent study of saffron DNA conducted in various regions (Europe and Israel) using the Random Amplifier Polymorphic DNA (RAPD) method has confirmed this observation, as it did not detect significant genomic differences among the samples. However, clear morphological differences have been observed between the different regions.

Saffron belongs to the family Iridaceae and is the most well-known member of the genus Crocus, which comprises about 85 species distributed worldwide. Crocus sativus is the only species in the Crocus genus that has received particular attention and cultivation in various countries. It is a small-sized plant with a globular underground bulb.

The peculiarity of this plant is its ability to bloom directly from the bulbs, earning it the name "isterantia."

The genus Crocus belongs to the phylum Angiosperms, the class Monocotyledons, the order Asparagales, and the family Iridaceae.

The family Iridaceae comprises perennial herbaceous plants with rhizomes, bulbs, or bulb-tubers. They have simple or branched stems and linear or pointed leaves, sheathing, with entire margins and parallel veins. The flowers are showy and enclosed by young leaves in a spathe with 2 or more bracts. The perianth consists of 6 tepals fused at the base or forming a more or less elongated tube that widens at the terminal part. The ovary has three locules containing many ovules, and the fruits are capsules containing numerous usually elongated seeds.

The genus Crocus includes about 80 species, most of which are distributed in the Mediterranean region, with some species extending to central Europe and central Asia. This genus exhibits a wide cytological variability, with an almost continuous series of chromosome numbers. The presence of B chromosomes, aneuploidy, and polyploid series is frequent, which could explain the segregation of local species, some of which may not have been fully analyzed in the Italian territory yet.

In the genus Crocus, many species are distinguished from Crocus sativus by the color of their flowers or the length of their stigmas compared to the stamens. These species are often ornamental plants with limited economic interest, but sometimes they are used to adulterate commercial saffron.

The spring-flowering species of the genus Crocus include:

- Crocus imperati

- Crocus suaveolens

- Crocus versicolor

- Crocus minimum

- Crocus corsicus

- Crocus albiflorus

- Crocus napolitanus

- Crocus etruscus

The autumn-flowering species of the genus Crocus include:

- Crocus thomasii

- Crocus medium

- Crocus longiflorus

- Crocus reticulatus

- Crocus biflorus

- Crocus weldenii

Crocus in Europe

Below is listed the variety of Crocus species reported in Flora Europaea vol. 5 (Tutin et al., 1980) along with the countries where their presence has been confirmed:

1. Crocus alatavicus - Turkey, Central Asia

2. Crocus albiflorus - Italy, France

3. Crocus ancyrensis - Turkey

4. Crocus angustifolius - Spain

5. Crocus antalyensis - Turkey

6. Crocus asumaniae - Turkey

7. Crocus banaticus - Balkans

8. Crocus biflorus - Balkan Peninsula

9. Crocus boryi - Turkey

10. Crocus byzantinus - Turkey, Greece, Albania

11. Crocus cancellatus - Iberian Peninsula

12. Crocus caspius - Caucasus, Iran

13. Crocus chrysanthus - Balkans, Greece, Turkey

14. Crocus cyprius - Cyprus

15. Crocus danfordiae - Turkey, Syria, Lebanon

16. Crocus danicus - Scandinavia

17. Crocus dispathaceus - Greece, Turkey

18. Crocus etruscus - Italy

19. Crocus flavus - Balkans, Greece, Turkey

20. Crocus gargaricus - Turkey

21. Crocus hadriaticus - Italy, Croatia, Albania

22. Crocus heuffelianus - Balkans

23. Crocus imperati - Italy

24. Crocus ibericus - Iberian Peninsula, Morocco

25. Crocus ilgazensis - Turkey

26. Crocus inouei - Balkan Peninsula, Greece, Turkey

27. Crocus istanbulensis - Turkey

28. Crocus karduchorum - Turkey

29. Crocus kotschyanus - Turkey, Iran

30. Crocus laevigatus - Turkey

31. Crocus ligusticus - Italy

32. Crocus longiflorus - Turkey, Syria

33. Crocus malyi - Ukraine

34. Crocus minimus - Iberian Peninsula

35. Crocus niveus - Turkey, Syria, Lebanon

36. Crocus olivieri - Turkey

37. Crocus oreocreticus - Greece

38. Crocus pallasii - Caucasus

39. Crocus pannonicus - Central Europe

40. Crocus paschei - Turkey

41. Crocus pelistericus - Balkan Peninsula

42. Crocus pestalozzae - Italy

43. Crocus pusillus - Central Europe, Balkans

44. Crocus reticulatus - Italy

45. Crocus robertianus - Italy, Croatia, Slovenia

46. Crocus romieuxii - Turkey, Syria, Lebanon, Palestine

47. Crocus rossicus - Crimea, Ukraine

48. Crocus sativus - Mediterranean, Balkans, Central Europe

49. Crocus serotinus - Iberian Peninsula

50. Crocus sieberi - Balkans, Greece, Turkey

51. Crocus sieheanus - Turkey

52. Crocus speciosus - Iberian Peninsula, Italy, Greece, Balkans

53. Crocus tommasinianus - Balkans, Italy, Hungary

54. Crocus tournefortii - Turkey

55. Crocus vallicola - Turkey

56. Crocus vernus - Central Europe, Balkans, Italy

57. Crocus vitellinus - Turkey

Please note that some of these species names may have been subject to revisions or updates since the publication, so it is always good to refer to updated botanical sources for further information.

Biological cycle

Saffron exhibits a biological cycle characterized by a long summer dormancy followed by active vegetative growth in autumn, during which flowers are formed, and a less intense activity during winter. During the summer, the plant endures adverse conditions by shedding its leaves and entering a quiescent state as a bulb-tuber. This bulb-tuber is compact, devoid of scales and bracts, and has a subovoid, flattened shape with a slight concavity at the base and convexity at the distal end. The size of the bulb-tuber varies from 1 to 5 cm in diameter and is covered by fibrous remains, weakly reticulated, of the leaf bases. Each year, the bulb-tuber undergoes renewal to support the development of the basal part of the flowering stem, thus enabling the autumn flowering of the plant.

The differentiation in the apex of the flower buds occurs during the period from the end of winter to spring, coinciding with a gradual attenuation of the harsh winter conditions. This period is of great importance as it significantly influences the production of the following year.

Once the development phase is completed, the plant ceases vegetative activity as the leaves dry up. At this point, the buds, starting from the main bud and following a decreasing sequence for the secondary buds, have already formed the primordia of the shoots, which will give rise to the flowers during the subsequent vegetative regrowth in autumn.

The life cycle of saffron follows a peculiar growth pattern

and is divided into three phases: flowering, vegetative phase, and bulb formation. In India, flowering occurs during autumn, from October to November, followed by the vegetative phase during winter and bulb formation, which takes place at the base of the shoots. When the dry period begins, from April to May, the leaves age and wither, and the bulbs enter a dormant state.

The transition from the vegetative phase to the reproductive phase occurs shortly after in the apex of the underground bulb sprouts. However, the timing of these events can vary significantly in different regions. For example, in Azerbaijan, the transition occurs in March, in Israel from March to April, and in Kashmir in July.

Differences in bulb size and seasonal variations are considered the causes of the differences in the plant's transition dates. This can lead to different practices in bulb harvesting, which may take place in May (as a common practice in many regions of Sardinia), the first rains of August, or during the period between early September and early October. During this time, the bulb-tubers can be kept out of the ground for a short period, ranging from a few days to a maximum of three months.

After the summer, the plant resumes vegetative growth, producing a tuft of leaves and the emergence of a floral stem wrapped in whitish bracts. Flowering occurs in autumn, between late October and mid-November. The flowers are showy, with 6 tepals of pinkish-purple color, as described earlier. From them, a stigma of bright red color emerges, divided into 3 branches, each ending in a trumpet-like structure. These stigmas are attached to the ovary through a long style.

During this same autumn-spring period, the leaves continue to grow, reaching a length of up to 40 cm, and the process of root development, resorption of the mother bulb, and the formation and growth of daughter bulbs occur simultaneously.

Each newly formed bulb-tuber, enclosed by the tunics of the bulb that produced it, has one or two main buds at the apex (from which new leaves, the floral axis, and one or two daughter bulb-tubers will originate), and 4-5 secondary buds below, arranged irregularly in a spiral. From these secondary buds, a sprout develops with a cauline axis and a group of leaves. At the base of the sprout, there is a bulb-tuber that, through the photosynthesis of the leaves, obtains nutrients and grows. Due to the presence of both apical buds (typical of bulbs) and secondary buds in various parts of the underground stem (typical of tubers), it seems more appropriate, for saffron, to use the term "bulb-tuber".

The bulb-tuber derived from the secondary buds is significantly smaller (about 1/4 - 1/6 of the size) compared to those produced by the apical buds. In this way, from each "mother" bulb, 2-3 main bulbs develop from the activity of the apical bud, and numerous secondary bulbs form from the lateral buds. Saffron reproduces vegetatively, through the mother bulb, by the growth and differentiation of both the main (apical) and secondary buds.

The pattern of growth and development in saffron - where

it loses its above-ground parts completely during the summer and remains in a geophytic quiescent phase - demonstrates that the plant is ecologically adapted to regions where the summer temperature does not fall below 25°C (monthly seasonal average) and the summer precipitation ranges from 20-40 mm.

In perennial plants, leaf emergence begins in the autumn, about two weeks earlier than in annual cycle plants. The period from March to April sees the greatest increase in the length of the leaf apparatus, with leaves reaching lengths of up to 40 cm. However, already in May, there is a progressive wilting of the leaves. During the period from March to April, vegetative activity is particularly intense, allowing the accumulation of reserve materials in the new bulb-tubers formed from the bulb-tuber that flowered in the previous year. This leads to their enlargement, which stops as summer approaches when the plant enters a state of rest and loses all its leaves and roots.

REQUIREMENTS

Saffron is a plant with low demands in terms of climate and can be successfully cultivated in various environmental conditions. Its geographic distribution extends between 10° West and 80° East longitude, and between 30° and 50° North latitude. Although it is native to Mediterranean countries, saffron is also successfully grown in other regions of the world.

In Italy, saffron cultivation has shown to yield good results at altitudes ranging from 650 to 1100 meters above sea level. However, the plant can also flower at higher elevations, such as at 2140 meters above sea level in Kashmir, India. Saffron can be cultivated in temperate, semi-arid, and arid zones, at altitudes ranging from 1500 to 2800 meters above sea level.

Diverse sources indicate optimal altitudes for saffron flowering, such as 1500-2000 meters above sea level or 1300-2500 meters above sea level. In any case, the plant shows remarkable adaptability and growth capabilities in various climatic conditions and altitudes.

Saffron thrives best in warm subtropical climates, where flowering occurs without frost and excessive rainfall. However, it also exhibits good resistance to low winter temperatures. On the other hand, extremely cold temperatures during the short flowering period can negatively affect flower production. If temperatures drop to -10/-15 °C, the bulb-tubers may suffer from splitting, leading to rapid decay of the plant.

Despite these delicacies, there are bibliographic references to saffron productions obtained in extreme climatic conditions, such as winter temperatures reaching -18°C and snowfall during flowering. Temperature plays a crucial role in regulating the development and flowering of saffron, and the presence of a consistent temperature is of considerable importance for the formation of its flowers.

It is interesting to note that the average annual temperature in saffron cultivation areas varies from 5.9°C to 18.6°C, while precipitation can range from 420 to 1370 mm in different regions. These climatic variations among different cultivation zones can significantly influence the growth and production of saffron.

The induction of saffron flowering occurs when the temperature reaches values above 20°C during late spring. However, the actual appearance of flowers happens when the temperature drops below 16°C. Studies conducted by Plessner have shown that it is possible to induce early flowering of saffron by placing the bulbs in dry vermiculite at 15°C for 35 days, followed by transferring them to controlled conditions in a growth chamber with a moist growth medium, a 16-hour photoperiod, and temperatures of 17°C during the day and 12°C at night.

The optimal temperature for flower formation has been found to be between 23°C and 27°C, with 23°C being slightly more favorable. To obtain the maximum number of flowers, incubation at these temperatures should last for more than 50 days, although prolonged incubation beyond 150 days has resulted in flower loss. The appearance of flowers occurs after transferring the bulbs from flower-forming conditions to a lower temperature of about 17°C.

Studies have also revealed that incubating the bulbs at higher temperatures, such as 30°C, reduces flower appearance and may cause the loss of some already emerged flowers. On the other hand, incubating the bulbs at 9°C did not result in flower formation. It has been observed that directly incubating the bulbs at 17°C, without prior incubation at 23-27°C, led to the formation of a single flower in a variable portion of the bulbs (ranging from 20% to 100%).

These findings suggest that ambient temperature plays a crucial role in the different phenological stages of saffron, influencing flowering, bulb development, and flower formation. In particular, temperatures between 23°C and 27°C seem to favor a higher flower production.

Atmospheric conditions, especially in the month of December, have a greater impact on bulb production rather than their size.

In the temperate and dry region of Himachal Pradesh, India, characterized by temperatures between 12°C and 18°C during the day and 4°C to 5°C at night in September and October, ideal conditions for saffron cultivation are found. Cloudy nights promote a higher flower production the following morning, while rains between August and September stimulate early flowering, increasing overall production. Dry and moderately humid climatic conditions during flowering are considered ideal for successful cultivation. On the contrary, frost during the flowering period can significantly hinder production and have a negative impact on productivity.

In Palampur, the average temperature in the months of September and October ranges between 19°C and 23°C, while in November and December, it drops to 8-13°C (data relative to a 30-year average), making it ideal for saffron cultivation.

High summer temperatures are not a problem for cultivation, while autumn frosts and early snowfalls pose a threat when the plant is in full bloom. If the flowers experience freezing temperatures, the bulb-tubers can easily rot and decay.

In Spain, saffron cultivation mainly occurs in dry areas, with rainfall rarely exceeding 400 mm per year. Winter temperatures oscillate between 3-5°C, while in summer, they can reach 25°C. In the Mediterranean region of Sardinia, the climate is milder, with rainfall concentrated mainly during the autumn-winter period. Winters are not very harsh, while summers are dry and hot. Precipitation averages around 560 mm per year, and average temperatures range from 10°C in winter to 25°C in summer. In Navelli, Italy, the cultivations extend to altitudes ranging from 650 m to 1100 m above sea level, with approximately 700 mm of precipitation and average temperatures oscillating between 11°C in winter and 20-22°C in summer. In Macedonia, the climate is similar to Spain, but the precipitation is almost doubled, reaching 700 mm.

As for rainfall, those in the month of March are particularly favorable during the formation of stems inside the bulb-tubers. September rains, as long as the soil has good drainage, are also beneficial as they allow the flowers to sprout quickly, anticipating the flowering.

Saffron has a development cycle of about 220 days. Saffron production is better in climates similar to those of the Mediterranean region, where warm and dry summer breezes blow over arid and semi-arid lands. However, the plant can also withstand cold winters, surviving frosts of -10°C and short periods of snow.

In conclusion, the best climatic conditions for the development and yield of saffron include a rainy autumn, a hot and dry summer, and a mild winter. The photoperiod, which is the duration of day and night, significantly influences the flowering of saffron, and an optimal lighting period of 10-11 hours is desirable. Saffron plants thrive under direct sunlight and perform poorly in shady environments. Therefore, cultivation is more successful in fields exposed to sunlight, preferably facing south in the northern hemisphere. Bryan reported that crocuses bloom in full sun as well as partial shade, but shaded areas should still receive at least 4 hours of sun per day.

The onset of saffron flowering appears to be influenced by the combination of temperature and soil moisture, while the flowering schedule seems independent of the bulb's origin, the surrounding environment, and plant density. On the other hand, the studied environmental factors strongly affect both the total stigmata yield and the qualitative characteristics. For example, a cooler environment may increase flower production, but it can negatively impact the quality of the stigmata.

The storage conditions of Crocus sativus bulbs have been studied in order to delay flowering. It has been observed that storing the bulbs at 2°C after the onset of flowering led to the loss of already emerged flowers. Furthermore, the more advanced the flowering initiation phase at the beginning of cold storage, the faster the loss of flowers occurred. In general, there was no benefit from storing the bulbs after the start of flowering.

The number and size of flowers formed per bulb depended on both the duration and the storage conditions. Storage at freezing temperatures (0° or -1°C) caused damage to the bulbs, but flowering was induced in bulbs stored between 0.5° and 25°C. Between these two values, the temperature had a limited impact on the subsequent behavior of the bulbs. The quantity and size of flowers gradually decreased with increasing storage duration. This decrease was slower when storage was carried out in an atmosphere with 1% oxygen compared to a normal atmosphere with 21% oxygen.

It was possible to induce flowering in bulbs collected after leaf withering and stored at 2°C in an atmosphere with 1% oxygen for 70 days, with the same yield as bulbs not stored in cold storage. These results, along with previous research, have demonstrated that it is possible to achieve saffron flowering without loss of yield from early September to the end of January. However, flowering could be further delayed until May by prolonging the duration of storage in cold storage, although this would result in a significant reduction in the production of dried stigmas.

The fundamental thermal conditions for the development of buds and flower formation in the Crocus sativus species, saffron, have been established. During late winter or spring, depending on the location, the plant's leaves showed withering, coinciding with an increase in temperature. In the first 30 days following leaf withering, no noticeable development was observed in the buds, neither in the underground bulbs nor in those already collected and placed in incubation in the laboratory under controlled conditions.

However, shortly after the withering of the leaves, flowering began, taking place during late spring or early summer when the temperature increased to around 20°C. If the summer was particularly hot and prolonged, the appearance of the flowers was delayed and occurred in late autumn when the temperature dropped to 15-17°C.

The physical properties of the soil play an essential role in supporting plant growth. These properties influence the relationship between the plant and the soil in terms of water and nutrient absorption, aeration, root penetration, and also regulate the soil temperature, activating microorganisms.

Among the physical properties of the soil, its composition is particularly relevant as it affects the soil structure, porosity, and permeability, as well as the water retention and drainage capacity. These factors are crucial for the growth and productivity of plants, especially in the case of bulbous plants like saffron.

In saffron cultivation, the bulbs not only constitute the main source of propagation but their size also significantly influences flower production per plant. Therefore, selecting suitable soil is essential to achieve a good yield in saffron cultivation.

For saffron cultivation, a sandy-loamy soil that is light and well-draining is preferred, as cold and wet soils can hinder proper bulb-tuber reproduction and promote their decomposition. Additionally, soils exposed to sunlight, well-aerated, and without overhanging trees are ideal for saffron growth. The presence of loose, calcareous soils with a good organic content further supports the development of the crop.

The physical properties of the soil are essential factors for the development and productivity of saffron. Compact and peaty soil can favor vegetative growth at the expense of reproductive development, negatively affecting the quality of the products. On the other hand, alkaline soil is considered ideal for achieving higher yields.

Different sources provide slightly different indications regarding the preferred soil type for saffron. Some authors suggest that the crop requires soil ranging from sandy to sandy-loamy. In Azerbaijan, saffron is successfully cultivated on sandy soils. Other experts recommend well-drained and clayey-limestone soils as more suitable for achieving optimal performance.

Regarding the soil pH, a value between 6.8 and 7.8 is considered optimal, while highly alkaline or siliceous soils are considered unsuitable. Some suggest that saffron prefers siliceous-clayey-iron-rich-gypsum soils, while others maintain that it can grow successfully on various types of soils, provided good drainage and proper cultivation practices are ensured.

It is important to avoid excessively wet soils as they can cause bulb decomposition. However, an adequate presence of calcium carbonate in the soil is considered favorable for good yields.

In conclusion, choosing the right soil is crucial for successful saffron cultivation, and well-drained, light, clayey-limestone soils with a pH between 6.8 and 7.8 appear to be the preferred conditions for achieving the best results.

Cultivation

Saffron cultivation can be carried out on an annual cycle, as is the case in Italy, particularly in Navelli, or on a perennial cycle, as it occurs in many traditionally saffron-producing countries. The duration of the perennial cycle can vary significantly from country to country: 3-4 years in Spain, 4-5 years in Sardinia, 6-8 years in India and Greece. In France, old plantations are replaced after 3 years due to the decrease in saffron yield caused by an excess of bulbs, making cultivation economically unviable. In Spain, on the other hand, bulbs are removed every four years. The choice of the duration of the perennial cycle is influenced by various factors, including climatic conditions, soil, agricultural practices, and plantation management.

Souret e Weathers conducted a comparison among three saffron cultivation systems: aeroponic, hydroponic, and soil-based. They found that bulb growth in terms of dry weight was higher in aeroponic and hydroponic cultures, but saffron stigma production and the concentration of major saffron constituents were similar in all three cultivation systems.

Omidbaigi and others studied the effect of cultivation locations on saffron quality in Iran. They observed that the quantity and quality of saffron (except for aroma) in the Neishabor region (North Khorasan) were better than those produced in the Ferdows region (South Khorasan).

In Iran, Keyhani and others cultivated saffron under different environmental conditions: in pots using field cultivation soil, in a semi-liquid agar-agar medium, and in a liquid medium. They noticed that root elongation was four times greater in the soil compared to the liquid environment.

Cavusoglu e Erkel studied the possibility of cultivating saffron under plastic tunnels and in open field conditions in the province of Kocaeli, Turkey. They obtained larger bulb sizes and a longer flowering period with the plastic tunnel, but a higher yield of saffron stigma (both fresh and dry) in the open field.

Many studies have confirmed the efficiency of soilless systems for saffron production. They investigated the effect of different substrates (peat and perlite) and environmental conditions (cold greenhouse and air-conditioned chamber). Perlite showed a higher saffron yield compared to the peat/perlite mixture. The productions obtained in the cold greenhouse and air-conditioned chamber were twice as high as traditional field cultivation.

Crop rotation and intercropping

Saffron cultivation requires special attention regarding the choice of soil and crop rotation practices. In several saffron-producing countries such as Spain, India, Greece, and Italy, it is customary to avoid planting saffron in the same soil in close succession. In the Navelli Plateau (L'Aquila), where saffron cultivation has a centuries-old tradition, it is customary to wait at least a decade before replanting saffron in the same plot, as a decrease in production has been observed. This phenomenon could be caused by the presence of toxins in the soil, giving rise to the concept of "soil fatigue." Furthermore, repeated monoculture may promote the onset of infections due to different pathogens, such as fusarium or viruses.

To improve crop rotation, cover crops such as weeds or wheat can be used before replanting saffron. In India, some intercropping practices, such as with almond trees, can be employed to take advantage of their early defoliation, which exposes saffron plants to sunlight.

Numerous studies have investigated the intercropping of saffron with other crops. In Kashmir (India), it has been shown that intercropping saffron with Damascus rose was successful compared to other intercropping systems or monoculture of the rose. In the temperate and dry conditions of Sangla (Himachal Pradesh, India), intercropping saffron with kalazira (Bunium persicum), a spice, outperformed other intercropping with kidney bean, bean, and mustard, as there was no competition between saffron and kalazira.

Furthermore, it has been observed that saffron can be successfully grown near apricot or almond trees. The almond trees shed their leaves before the active growth period of saffron, contributing to better light penetration on the cultivated plants. However, saffron cultivation in the orchard is only feasible during the initial growth stages of the tree.

In Kashmir, India, farmers practice crop rotation of saffron with cereals such as wheat and mustard. Typically, saffron is continuously cultivated for 8-10 years in the same field and then followed by a sequence of wheat, barley, and oilseed crops before being replanted (i.e., it is replanted after a gap of 4 years).

Planting

The planting period of saffron varies from region to region, depending on the climatic and soil characteristics of the environment in which it is cultivated and the duration of the production cycle. Research has shown that the best timing for planting bulbs varies depending on the location.

For example, in some regions of India, such as Almora (Uttar Pradesh), mid-July has been found to be the best time for planting bulbs, while in Crimea, USSR, for plants with autumn flowering, late August to mid-September has been identified as the optimal time. In Pakistan, in the Baluchistan region, higher yields were obtained by planting from mid-July, but yields were lower when planting in August or June.

In Iran, it has been established that the best time for planting and relocating saffron bulbs in new farms is from mid-May to early June. In Italy, saffron is planted in the second half of August, while in Spain, it is preferred to plant between June 15 and June 30, and in Greece, before mid-September. The planting timings influence the production of cormlets per mother corm: in India, planting on November 15 and December 1 produces many more cormlets compared to planting on December 16.

It should be noted that in polycyclic crops, the planting period tends to be earlier than the period adopted in annual cultivation. This temporal variation aims to optimize the production cycle and environmental conditions to achieve a better saffron yield.

Soil preparation

Soil preparation is a fundamental aspect to ensure the successful growth of saffron. Depending on the pedoclimatic conditions, the soil is worked multiple times during the summer and autumn months of the year preceding the planting, to a depth of about 30-35 cm. In Spain, such as in the region of Castilla La Mancha, it is advisable to perform the main soil preparations in March-April to take advantage of the spring rains. However, these operations can also be carried out in May-June, shortly before planting the bulbs.

After soil preparation, the next step involves amending the soil and removing weeds. In some areas, it is customary to create ridges that are 1.2-1.5 meters wide and 15-20 centimeters high. Between the ridges, pathways around 30 centimeters wide can be established, which also serve as drainage channels to prevent waterlogging in the top 15-20 centimeters of the soil. However, in sandy or sandy-loamy soils and in dry temperate regions with low-intensity rainfall, ridge formation may not be necessary.

Towards the end of winter, it is advisable to carry out an organic fertilization by incorporating the material to a medium depth (around 150-200 quintals per hectare), preferably using sheep-origin fertilizers. This operation can be performed through plowing or with a second shallower plowing, which also allows for weed control. In the late spring, if new weeds are observed, it is recommended to perform one or more harrowings to keep them under control.

Polycyclic cultivation (Spain-Greece-India)

In Spain, saffron planting follows a specific procedure. In the plot of land, deep furrows of about 20 cm and 10-15 cm wide are created so that the bulbs do not emerge on the surface during the subsequent years of cultivation. The results obtained show that by planting the bulbs at a depth of 20 cm, a yield of approximately 3 kg/ha/year is achieved, a significantly higher figure compared to cultivation at 10 cm depth.

In the first two years of cultivation (year zero and year 1), the yield at 10 cm depth is higher compared to that obtained at 20 cm depth. However, from the third flowering onwards (year 2), the trend reverses, and the yield becomes higher with planting at 20 cm depth. From this point onwards, the results continue to favor planting at greater depth.

The distance between the furrows generally varies from 30 to 40 cm, ensuring sufficient space for the next planting and facilitating product harvesting. The digging of the furrows can be done manually or with the help of a small plow, shaping the furrow to obtain a rectangular section.

In Greece, the cultivation operations are similar, but the furrows are closer together, with a distance of about 20-25 cm, while maintaining the same depth as in Spain. In both countries, mounds are not used as the reduced rainfall does not require special attention to water drainage.

In India, where saffron cultivation is polyennial, and precipitation can be abundant, mounds are instead used.

This technique involves creating drainage ditches around small mounds (about 2.5 square meters). Within these areas, parallel furrows, 12-14 cm wide and 10 cm deep, are opened, with a different ratio between productive surface and cultivated surface.

When the furrows are opened using the plow, the soil from one furrow is used to cover the previously opened one, and at the end of planting, the ground is leveled by operating transversely to the direction of the furrows.

Recently, specially modified agricultural machines, similar to potato planters, have been experimented with, and they have yielded satisfactory results. These machines are equipped with two rear hillers that cover the furrows.

MICROPROPAGATION

Micropropagation or in vitro propagation is a vegetative propagation technique used for the growth and multiplication of plants in a controlled environment, with optimal conditions of light, temperature, and nutrients. The microplants are cultivated in a specially formulated gel that contains all essential nutrients, such as mineral salts, vitamins, and sucrose, along with hormonal substances necessary for growth.

Maintaining sterility is a fundamental requirement in this process, as the culture media used could encourage the growth of unwanted bacteria and fungi.

Micropropagation offers numerous advantages, including the ability to produce large quantities of homogeneous material (clones) in a rapid and controlled manner, preserving the genetic characteristics of the mother plants. Additionally, the plants can be continuously propagated throughout the year, eliminating the dependence on traditional propagation methods such as cuttings or seasonal grafting. In vitro techniques also allow the elimination of any diseases present in the starting material and maintain the health characteristics during subsequent multiplication cycles. This technique is particularly useful for propagating plants that are difficult to propagate using traditional methods. Therefore, in vitro culture represents a powerful tool for nursery production and genetic-sanitary certification of plants.

In addition to being a highly efficient method for plant multiplication, micropropagation plays a vital role in the conservation of biodiversity, the enhancement of productions, and the protection of the environment.

One of the significant applications of micropropagation is the use of microshoots for cryopreservation, an innovative technique that allows the preservation of genetic resources. By freezing shoots, meristems, whole seeds, or embryos at extremely low temperatures, such as liquid nitrogen (-196°C), it is possible to keep the plant material safe from contamination and genetically unchanged for a virtually unlimited period.

Micropropagation also finds application in the reproduction of medicinal plants, biomass production, and the cultivation of mycorrhizal plants. These applications have the dual purpose of protecting the environment and integrating farmers' income.

The process of micropropagation involves several stages:

1. Induction and stabilization of cultures in an aseptic environment to ensure the purity of the starting material.

2. Promotion of regenerative activity and multiplication of new shoots through the use of appropriate hormonal substances and culture conditions.

3. Induction and development of new roots at the base of the shoots to facilitate their growth and rooting.

4. Transplantation and acclimatization of micropropagated plants to external environments, allowing them to gradually adapt to natural conditions.

Micropropagation begins with the careful selection of plant

material intended for propagation. The choice and cleaning of this material are crucial to obtain healthy and contamination-free plants. Typically, the plants undergo tests to ensure their "cleanliness," meaning the absence of viruses, fungi, and contaminating bacteria.

The concept of cell totipotency is fundamental to the success of this technique. The explants (portions of the plant taken for in vitro culture) used for micropropagation can be divided into two categories:

1. The first category includes explants that contain preformed meristematic structures, such as apical tips, buds, and nodes. These regions of the plant have a high capacity for cell multiplication and regeneration.

2. The second category includes explants consisting of differentiated tissues, such as leaf segments, stems, roots, or flowers. In this case, the regenerative capacity is lower compared to explants containing meristems.

In the first category of explants, it is rare for the resulting plants to be genetically different from the original, while in the second category, especially when the plants originate from callus (aggregates of undifferentiated cells), somaclonal variations can occur more frequently, giving rise to genetic variability. This variability is used in plant breeding as it represents a tool to increase genetic diversity.

Once the base material is selected, the collection of explants from the mother plant can begin depending on the chosen micropropagation technique. Before starting in vitro culture, it is essential to perform a careful external cleaning of the plant material to remove any macroscopic pests, followed by sterilization using agents such as alcohol, bleach, etc., to eliminate microscopic parasites, such as fungi and bacteria, that may be present on the plant's surface.

The small piece of plant tissue used, sometimes just a single cell, is transferred under sterile conditions onto a culture medium. The culture media serve as the primary source of nutrients for the explants and are either liquid solutions or solidified with gelling agents like agar or other compounds. These culture media contain sucrose as an energy source, macroelements (N, P, K, Ca, Mg, S), and essential mineral microelements for growth (Fe, Cu, Zn, Mn, Co, Ni, Al, Na, Mo, I, Cl). They also include one or more growth regulators (plant hormones), and sometimes vitamins, amino acids, and other substances like antioxidants (e.g., citric acid, ascorbic acid) and adsorbent compounds (such as activated charcoal, PVP polymer that absorbs phenols). Agar is the most commonly used and expensive gelling agent, followed by other cost-effective gelling agents like pectin and gelrite (which requires smaller doses compared to agar). The culture media can also be liquid or maintained in semi-immersed equipment.

To prevent contamination from fungi and bacteria, the culture media are sterilized during preparation. This process eliminates potential contaminants and helps ensure an aseptic environment for the growth of explants. The commonly used methods for sterilization are autoclaving and filtration sterilization.

The plant tissue grows and differentiates into new tissues depending on the variations, primarily in the phytohormones, present in the culture media used. The main categories of phytohormones used in in vitro culture are:

1. AUXINS (such as IAA, IBA, NAA, 2,4D): These phytohormones can induce the differentiation of adventitious roots, stimulate callus formation (formation of undifferentiated cells), and somatic embryogenesis.

2. CYTOKININS (such as K, 2iP, Zeatin, BAP, Thidiazuron): Cytokinins promote cell division, induce the formation of new shoots, and stimulate the growth of shoot apices.

3. GIBBERELLINS: Gibberellins stimulate cell elongation, promote internode elongation, and enhance shoot growth.

It is important to note that gibberellic acid is sensitive to high temperatures.

The shoots grown in vitro are heterotrophic, which means they obtain sugars directly from the culture medium and fix only a small amount of CO_2. This is different from plants under normal conditions, which utilize photosynthesis to produce their energy. In in vitro culture, the nutrients provided in the culture medium support the growth and development of the plants since they cannot independently produce their own nutrients.

Preparation and planting of bulbs

The bulb-tubers to be used for cultivation are collected from different plots of land, which cannot be reused for 8-10 years, as already specified earlier. To extract them from the soil, a lateral furrow is made next to the old planting area at an appropriate depth (approximately 15-20 cm) to avoid damaging them with the plow.

The bulb-tubers emerge wrapped in fibrous sheaths of reddish-brown color, with bright basal residues of leaf vascular bundles. They are present in compact groups, consisting of three or more bulb-tubers of varying sizes, closely connected to the mother bulb, indicating their origin. Throughout its vegetative cycle, the cultivation will produce a large number of bulb-tubers, depending on its duration in the soil.

After harvesting, the bulb-tubers are roughly cleared of soil and prepared for the sorting phase. Sorting the bulb-tubers involves the careful removal of old tuber residues, soil, and any deformed or parasite-affected parts, both animal and plant-related. Additionally, the bulb-tubers are separated based on their sizes, with particular attention given to those with a diameter less than 3 cm, which will be planted separately.

The sorted bulb-tubers are stored in a dry, well-ventilated, and dark environment, arranged in thin layers, until the time of replanting or their subsequent use. Proper storage is essential to maintain their quality and vitality.

Before proceeding with the replanting, the bulb-tubers can

undergo a cleaning of their outer tunics, although this step is often omitted to save time and labor. It is essential to ensure that the bulb-tubers are healthy, free from spots, wounds, or signs of decay.

To prevent the spread of fungal diseases, the bulb-tubers can be treated with a fungicide containing benomyl, by immersing them in a 5-10‰ solution for 15-20 minutes. Alternatively, in Spain and India, a 5% solution of copper sulfate can be used for disinfection. The necessity of such treatment may vary depending on local practices and soil conditions.

Once the planting of bulb-tubers is completed, it is important to level the surface of the soil with a leveler, a heavy board, or a light roller. Alternatively, for smaller areas, a simple rake can be used. This operation is recommended to ensure better soil adhesion to the bulb-tubers and to eliminate furrows that could cause abnormal water accumulation during heavy rainfall. Saffron cultivation is particularly sensitive to prolonged humidity.

In Spain, some studies indicate that the size of the bulb plays a determining role in the production in the planting year, as it influences the number of floral shoots. However, in the subsequent years, this factor gradually loses importance with the appearance of bulbils. Starting from the thirteenth year of flowering, no significant differences in yield are observed between bulbs of different sizes.

In Italy, during the selection of bulb-tubers, those with a diameter of approximately 2.5 cm or larger are separated from the rest. The smaller bulbs are still used but are placed in a nursery to allow them to grow over the next two or three years since they won't be able to bloom in the first year but will only produce leaves. The size of the bulbs used in Sardinia is generally larger than 2.5-3 cm. The smaller bulbs are planted randomly in a furrow dug at the border of the field.

Planting density

Planting density has a significant impact on the crop yield in the first year, but this influence diminishes in the following years. In the first year, the saffron yield is closely related to the number of floral shoots, which, in turn, depends on both the density of planted bulbs and the number of shoots per bulb, which is also influenced by the size of the bulbs.

The distance between bulbs is an important parameter and should be chosen based on the size of the production area, so as not to interfere with the development of adjacent bulbs. Planting techniques vary both in Italy and abroad. For example, one study reported that distances of 15 × 5 cm and 20 × 15 cm respectively provided the maximum and minimum number of flowers per square meter. In the temperate and dry conditions of Sangla, Himachal Pradesh (India), a distance of 20 × 20 cm is considered ideal for continuous production for 10 years. However, another study found that a distance of 10 × 7.5 cm between rows produces more in the initial years compared to 15 × 10 cm and 20 × 15 cm in Sangla, India. In Morocco, plots of 2 × 2 m with rows spaced 20 cm apart and with 2-3 bulbs planted at a distance of 10-15 cm within the rows have been used. In the Greek context, bulbs are planted in furrows created with a plow at a distance of 25 × 12 cm.

Ultimately, the choice of planting density and distance can vary depending on local pedoclimatic conditions, cultural practices, and production objectives. It is important to carefully consider these factors to achieve optimal yield over the years of cultivation.

The size of the bulb is a crucial factor that influences the flowering capacity and saffron production of bulbous plants. Previous studies have shown that larger bulbs have positive effects on overall production.

Indeed, larger bulbs, with a diameter ranging from 4-5 cm, allow for a greater production of flowers and daughter bulbs in the annual cycle. The more daughter bulbs produced, the greater the overall quantity of floral shoots present in the larger bulbs, promoting greater flowering.

Bulbs below a certain threshold size, such as 10 grams in weight, are not capable of producing flowers in the current year or in the following years. Therefore, planting large bulbs, with a diameter of about 4-5 cm, is crucial to achieve better yields. However, some studies have demonstrated that even bulbs with a diameter of 2.5 cm can produce flowers and bulblets.

Further research has highlighted that larger bulbs, measuring over 3.5 cm in diameter and weighing approximately 20g, have produced four times more flowers compared to smaller bulbs weighing only 10g. Similar studies have recorded the best flower productions from larger bulbs in various regions, such as India and Spain.

Additionally, it has been demonstrated that larger bulbs, ranging from 3.25-3.75 cm in diameter, exhibit longer stigmas, a higher number of flowers per bulb, longer leaves, and a greater number of daughter bulbs produced from the mother bulb. The use of larger bulbs, therefore, contributes to achieving higher yields and better overall results in the cultivation of this plant.

Fertilization

Fertilization is a fundamental aspect in saffron cultivation, although this plant has relatively low nutritional requirements. When harvesting saffron, including its leaves, significant amounts of nitrogen (N), phosphorus (P), and potassium (K) are taken from the soil. For instance, for every ton of harvested leaves, approximately 10.2 kg of nitrogen, 3.2 kg of phosphorus, and 22.8 kg of potassium are removed from the soil.

The use of organic fertilizers has proven to improve the physical condition and structure of the soil, enhancing its water retention capacity. The application of manure as a basal dressing is done in varying quantities depending on the region: from 15 to 22 tons per hectare in Ranikhet, 20 tons in Greece, 15-20 tons in Kashmir, 30 tons in Sangla, India, and 40 tons in Iran.

It should be emphasized that organic fertilization alone is not sufficient to fully meet the nutritional needs of saffron. Therefore, it is necessary to combine organic and mineral fertilizers to achieve higher yields. For instance, adding 30 tons of bovine manure and 50 kg of ammonium phosphate per hectare resulted in a significant increase in saffron production in nutrient-poor soils. In another location, the application of 100 kg of urea per hectare led to the highest flower yield.

Studies have shown that nitrogen had the most significant effect in promoting flower production, especially in sandy soils. Adding 20 tons of organic material along with 100 kg of a fertilizer containing N+P+K per hectare resulted in the highest saffron production.

Various research conducted in different environments has provided important findings regarding the best fertilization practices for saffron cultivation.

In sandy or sandy-loam soils in the Netherlands, the highest bulb yield has been demonstrated with an annual split application of 150 kg of nitrogen per hectare.

In rainy environments like Kashmir, different combinations of fertilizers have been suggested. Munshi et al. recommended applying 20 kg of nitrogen, 80 kg of phosphorus, and 20 kg of potassium at the time of sowing or before the final plowing, and then after flowering, along with 20 tons of organic matter per hectare. In this region, dosages of 30 kg of nitrogen and potassium and 40 kg of phosphorus per hectare have been found to be ideal. Higher dosages of nitrogen, phosphorus, and potassium (90 kg of nitrogen, 60 kg of phosphorus, and 60 kg of potassium per hectare) significantly increased saffron production in Sangla, India. However, in Kashmir, a significant increase in production was observed with the application of a medium level of nutrients (45-50-30 kg of nitrogen, phosphorus, and potassium per hectare) and a high amount of organic matter (20 tons per hectare).

L'interazione tra fosforo e potassio è un altro aspetto rilevante. Singh et al. hanno studiato questa interazione e ottenuto un aumento del 125.64% nella produzione di zafferano controllata applicando 35 kg di fosforo e 30 kg di potassio per ettaro a Kishtwar, India.

In Iran, è stato osservato un aumento del 33% nella resa dello zafferano applicando 46 chilogrammi di azoto per ettaro sotto forma di urea e 30 tonnellate di letame per ettaro. Inoltre, Hosseini et al. hanno segnalato che l'applicazione fogliare di fertilizzanti a base di azoto ha incrementato il numero di fiori del 33% quando effettuata nel mese di marzo.

Boynton ha evidenziato l'importanza della fertilizzazione fogliare per eliminare carenze di sostanze nutritive nelle piante orticole e nei prodotti agricoli. In particolare, l'applicazione di potassio è stata associata ad un aumento del contenuto di K e di clorofilla, del contenuto relativo di ATP (adenosina trifosfato) e del tasso fotosintetico netto delle foglie.

In Turkey, Unal and Cavusoglu studied the effects of different nitrogen-based fertilizers on saffron and reported that urea contributed to obtaining the highest number of flowers and the greatest weight of fresh and dry saffron, while ammonium nitrate influenced the maximum plant height.

These researches highlight the importance of proper fertilization to achieve high yields and improve the quality of saffron, both through the application of fertilizers to the soil and through foliar application.

Irrigation

In saffron cultivation, irrigation is generally not practiced because during periods of water scarcity, the bulb-tubers are in a dormant phase. However, it is important to note that the water requirements of saffron vary depending on the climatic conditions and the soil in which it is grown.

In Kashmir, where the annual rainfall is 1000-1500 mm, saffron is exclusively cultivated relying on rainwater. However, due to increasing water scarcity, saffron production in this region is declining.

In some regions, such as in Morocco, irrigation with 350-500 m³ of water per hectare is usually done once a week from September to November and every two weeks from December to March. During the months of April to August, which correspond to the dormant period of the bulb-tubers, no irrigation is performed.

In Iran, irrigation needs can vary and are estimated at around 3000 m³ per hectare annually, while in Morocco, they are around 500 m³, according to various sources.

Irrigation is particularly important in early spring for bulb development, while rainfall just before flowering can promote higher flower production. Additionally, adequate irrigation in the early months of autumn can accelerate flowering and improve the quantity and quality of the harvest.

In Spain, where the climate is temperate and dry with approximately 400 millimeters of annual rainfall, irrigation is practiced during saffron cultivation. In Greece, where the annual rainfall is about 500 millimeters, irrigation is also an important practice for achieving good yields.

In conclusion, saffron irrigation needs may vary depending on the region, but providing adequate water during crucial stages of cultivation can promote higher production and better quality of the final product.

Weeds

Weeds can be a significant problem in saffron cultivation, causing estimated losses between 5% and 20% of the harvest. Weed competition is particularly critical during the growing cycle, with notable differences depending on whether the crop is annual or perennial.

In fields cultivated annually, saffron reaches its maximum vegetative growth in March-April, when weed growth is usually limited. However, between May and July, when saffron enters a period of underground dormancy, weeds can reach their maximum development. In some regions, like the Navelli plateau, where the cultivation is traditionally annual, weed control is often neglected, and by the end of May or early June, the field is mowed to reduce weed growth.

On the other hand, in perennial cultivations, where the bulb-tubers remain in the ground for several years, it is essential to remove the weeds before the autumn germination. If the soil is not ridged, as is the case in some areas of Spain, shallow cross plowing or harrowing is performed to eliminate the weeds without damaging the bulb-tubers. During this process, manure is also incorporated to improve soil fertility.

The soil tillage, besides controlling weeds, also has the positive effect of keeping the soil fresh, which is important for saffron cultivation. These tillage operations are repeated until the month of September to keep weed growth under control.

In the case of ridged soil, where the soil is elevated in raised beds, shallow plowing is carried out using cultivators with surface tillage to avoid damaging the crop.

In conclusion, weed control is an essential practice in saffron cultivation, and the soil tillage techniques vary depending on the type of cultivation (annual or perennial) and the method of soil preparation (ridged or non-ridged). Proper weed management is crucial to ensure optimal yields and the health of saffron plants.

To reduce the need for manual or mechanical interventions for weed control, various mulching and ground covering methods have been studied. Among the materials used for mulching, better results have been obtained with wood derivatives such as wood chips, sawdust, and shavings. Some other tested options include polyethylene films, fern leaves and stems, rye straw, and wood chips.

In Greece, a traditional practice for weed control involved the use of animal trampling, mainly by mules and donkeys. These animals would repeatedly walk over the soil, up to three times, before early September, thus destroying the weeds. This method was supplemented by light plowing or harrowing, both before and after planting the bulbs. However, it is important that the soil tillage depth after planting does not exceed 8 - 10 cm, to prevent the bulbs from emerging from the soil or getting damaged.

In Sardinia, for weed control, tools like hoes are used for interventions along the planting lines. Additionally, motor cultivators are used for broader operations between the rows, such as weeding, harrowing, or hilling.

The use of mulching and green coverings can contribute to reducing the presence of weeds, making mechanical and manual weed control more efficient. Soil management practices may vary depending on specific local conditions and grower preferences. The goal is to maintain saffron cultivation healthy and reduce the negative impact of weeds on production.

Animal pest control

Saffron cultivation can be susceptible to damage caused by various types of pests and rodents. Among rodents, rats and voles may feed on the bulb-tubers, causing significant damage to the crop. Moles, on the other hand, create tunnels in the soil and are particularly attracted to bulb-tubers. Hares and mice can also cause damage to the above-ground part of the plant, especially the vegetative part. Additionally, mice and moles can cause considerable damage to the saffron crop by removing the bulbs. Even crows can cause damage to the flowering, resulting in a significant loss of flowers.

Another unusual pest that can attack the saffron flower is the blister beetle, which feeds on nectar and damages the flower's stigma. Additionally, Chandel and others have reported a new saffron pest, the blister beetle.

To protect the cultivation from pest and rodent attacks, various control measures can be adopted, including the use of physical barriers, repellents, traps, or biological control methods. It is essential to constantly monitor the cultivation for any signs of infestations and intervene promptly to prevent them from worsening. Integrated pest management, combining different control strategies, can help reduce damage and protect the saffron cultivation.

To counter predators such as rodents and moles that can damage saffron cultivation, several control measures are employed. One strategy involves preparing poisoned baits using toxic products like sodium arsenite, arsenic anhydride, strychnine, and zinc phosphide. These products are mixed with grains or chopped alfalfa and sprinkled on some fruits to attract rodents and predators.

However, it should be emphasized that the use of such products is extremely dangerous and must be handled with great caution. It is crucial to strictly follow usage instructions and adopt appropriate safety measures to protect both the environment and agricultural workers.

To counter moles and mice living in underground tunnels, another method used is the introduction of ignited fuses that produce toxic gases like burnt sulfur or straw mixed with sulfur. These gases are released inside the tunnels to eliminate the predators.

In Spain, an alternative used by farmers is the use of exhaust gases from motor-scooter tailpipes left running for a few hours. These gases are introduced inside the tunnels to eliminate the predators. It is essential to carry out these operations with care and caution to ensure the safety and success of the control measures.

Diseases of Saffron

The main problems that can affect saffron bulbs are usually related to the action of pathogenic fungi such as Fusarium oxysporum, Rhizoctonia croccorum, and Rhizoctonia violacea, in addition to the mite Rhizoglyphus. The presence of biotic agents can have a negative impact on saffron production.

Bulb rot represents the most severe disease for saffron and is caused by various types of fungi that develop in the soil, such as Rhizoctonia, Fusarium solani, Phoma crocophila, Macrophomina phaseolina, and a species of Basidiomycotina. Infected bulbs show spots of red, brown, black, or white coloration. In Italy, the presence of Macrophomina phaseolina was first reported by Carta. In India, Thakur and others have reported bulb rot caused by Macrophomina phaseolina with symptoms affecting 30-40% of the bulbs. This disease was observed during sowing.

The occurrence of Fusarium oxysporum gladioli on saffron has also been reported in Italy by Cappelli. Other Italian authors, such as Francesconi, have reported bulb rot in saffron caused by Penicillium cyclopium, especially during the hot and humid period between July and August. Furthermore, it has been observed that damaged bulbs are more susceptible to diseases.

The initial symptoms of decomposition appear during the flowering phase of saffron, with the yellowing and drying of the buds, caused by the wilting of the lower part of the stem and the appearance of white and round spots on the bulb. A dusty black patina forms under the outer layer of the bulb.

For the effective control of bulb rot caused by Fusarium oxysporum, some treatments have been developed. Shah and Srivastava achieved success in controlling the disease by using 80% captafol, carbendazim, or benomyl, each at 0.2%. The bulbs were immersed in these solutions for 20 minutes before planting. Additionally, the application of chemicals such as chlorpyrifos, carbofuran 10 G, or quinalphos 5 G, at a rate of 25-30 kg per hectare at the time of planting, proved effective in combating beetle larvae attacks.

Blooming and harvest

Saffron blooms in autumn, usually between the end of October and the end of November. However, the exact flowering period can vary due to different factors, such as temperature and rainfall conditions, the planting date of the crop, and the size and origin of the bulb-tubers used.

Moderate rains that occur at the end of summer or the beginning of autumn can promote earlier flowering. Flowering is significantly influenced by temperature and ambient humidity; warm or humid days tend to favor concentrated anthesis, while frost, snow, and cold can hinder it, leading to a more prolonged flowering period (usually around 20 days).

During the harvesting period, there is an abundant floral production, which can occur two or three times. The flowering pattern follows a Gaussian distribution, with an early onset and a prolonged duration compared to the peak flowering. This staggered flowering requires significant and continuous labor commitment during the harvesting period.

The timing of bulb-tuber planting has a significant impact on saffron flowering. In general, delaying the planting of bulbs tends to postpone the onset of plant anthesis. Therefore, in environments characterized by cold autumns, it is preferable to advance the saffron planting to promote earlier flowering.

The size and origins of bulb-tubers also influence the flowering of the saffron plants. Larger bulbs tend to have an earlier flowering, while differences of about 20 days have been observed between Spanish and Italian origins, with the latter showing earlier flowering.

The saffron flower harvesting is a delicate and crucial phase in the production of this precious spice. In saffron-producing countries, the harvesting is done in the early morning, preferably before the flower opens due to exposure to sunlight. Harvesting the still-closed flowers is quicker and facilitates the subsequent "thrumming" operation, which involves separating the stigmas from the tepals and stamens. This method ensures greater resistance of the floral organs against deterioration.

However, the harvesting and separation of the saffron stigmas from the flower are very labor-intensive and time-consuming operations. To produce one kilogram of dried saffron, several hundred hours of work are required, as 1000 flowers take approximately 45-55 minutes for harvesting and an additional 100-130 minutes for the separation of the stigmas. This makes saffron one of the most expensive spices in the world.

The harvesting begins shortly after dawn to avoid prolonged exposure to the sun, as heat and sunlight can cause rapid loss of color and flavor and wilting of the flowers. The flowers are collected at the base of the segments and arranged in baskets in thin layers to prevent damage to the floral organs, especially the stigmas.

Once harvested, the flowers are taken indoors for the separation of the stigmas. During this phase, stigmas shorter than 2 mm are separated from the rest of the floral organs. Stigmas longer than 2 mm are considered of lower quality.

Harvesting saffron is a delicate process influenced by weather conditions. During days of intense blooming, it is preferable to complete the harvest before the sun heats up the ground. Otherwise, the harvest can be done the previous evening. If the sky is cloudy, the harvest can be extended into the morning, while on cold days with frost, one must wait for the atmosphere to warm up to reduce the fragility of the flowers.

The harvest is carried out manually, as mechanization of this phase is still challenging. In Italy, where the terrain is ridged and divided into dosses (raised beds), the operator proceeds with the harvest of two rows at a time, alternating between the left and right alleys. In Spain, where the terrain is not ridged, the harvester can pick flowers from three adjacent rows with a single movement.

The yield of the harvest depends on the skills of the operator and the cultivation and weather conditions. An average yield of 8-16 kg of flowers per person per day is estimated. To pick the flower, it is necessary to grip it between the thumb and index finger of one hand and cut it with the thumbnail about one centimeter below the throat, which is the point where the flower's bell begins. The harvested flowers are then placed in wicker baskets to prevent them from being crushed. In case of a bountiful harvest, the flowers are dumped onto a cloth or sack and transferred to the processing facility for the subsequent "thrumming" operation, which involves separating the stigmas from the other parts of the flower.

In Greece, flower harvesting takes place daily between 9:00 AM and 5:00 PM. The flowers are carefully cut at the base of the petals, and harvesting occurs when the flower is fully open.

In Sardinia, harvesting usually takes place from the second half of October to the first half of November, while in Spain, the period is approximately the same as in Sardinia. In Greece, flower harvesting takes place from October 15th to 30th, while in India (Kashmir), it occurs in late autumn.

Regarding flower production, each bulb with a diameter greater than 2.5 cm produces 2 to 5 flowers. Flower production depends on various factors, such as climate conditions, soil type, and planting density. On average, from one hectare of saffron cultivation, 4-5 tons of fresh flowers are harvested, from which approximately 50 kg of stigmas are obtained after drying.

Mechanization of flower harvesting in saffron cultivation is not always feasible. It is only possible if the land has been properly prepared after planting or at the end of summer, in the case of a crop cultivated in previous years. In such cases, machinery like tillers are used to work the soil to a depth of 3 to 10 cm, depending on the position of the shoots. After turning the soil, it is leveled and compacted using a motorized roller. It is essential to clear the land from weeds and plant residues beforehand.

Productivity

Saffron can be cultivated with a multi-year cycle, which can last up to 10 years depending on the location, or with an annual cycle. Flower production is influenced by various variables, such as climatic and soil conditions, planting characteristics and density, the duration of the production cycle, and in the case of multi-year cultivation, the year of production.

The maximum yield occurs in the first two years (i.e., the second and third flowering), while from the third year onwards, production starts to decrease. For example, in the region of Western Macedonia, the annual saffron production averages around 10 kg/ha and is mainly dependent on the prevailing weather conditions in autumn. The amount of saffron harvested can vary from 1.5 to 15.0 kg/ha, depending on the sowing density, age of the plantation, and climatic conditions during the harvest season. Productivity data is typically expressed as yield per hectare of dried saffron.

In India, in the Kashmir region, the maximum recorded production has been 6.8 kg/ha, but this value has been influenced by a high incidence of defects (such as water and service dripping pits) compared to the productive surface. Other researches have reported lower yields, such as 3.8 kg/ha in temperate climatic conditions and 2.9 kg/ha in rainy climates in Kishtwar, India.

In Greece, the flower yield varies over time, ranging from 3 to 15 kg/ha. Values like 3.0 kg/ha in the first year, 10.0 kg/ha in the second year, 15.0 kg/ha in the third and fourth year, and a decrease to 10.0 kg/ha during the fifth and sixth year have been recorded. On average, one hectare of multi-year cultivation produces 60.0 kg of red saffron (stigma and styles) or 20.0 kg of yellow saffron (stamens) over 6 years.

In Spain, where the cultivation is multi-year in the Mancha region, the average production is around 10.0-12.5 kg/ha. However, under rainy conditions and inadequate fertilization in Kashmir, the production decreases to only 1.5-3.0 kg/ha.

The average saffron yield in Morocco varies from 2.0 to 2.5 kg/ha, which is considered low compared to modern saffron plantations in Spain or Italy. This is mainly due to the presence of rain and irrigation during bulb formation and plant development, which significantly reduces productivity. One kilogram of fresh flowers yields approximately 72 g of fresh saffron (stigmas), which, in turn, produce 12 g of dried stigmas. The final product retains a moisture content of about 5-20%.

In the Khorasan province of Iran, the average yield of commercial saffron fields is 4.4 kg/ha. In Navelli, Italy, the average production of dried saffron/ha is 10-16 kg. This area has recorded the highest saffron production/ha rate in the world.

In the Netherlands and Japan, saffron bulbs are produced and exported. De Juan et al. recorded a bulb production ranging from 28.4 to 36.3 tons per hectare in Spain.

In Italy, where saffron cultivation is annual, production

generally varies between 10 and 15 kg per hectare. Aquilano farmers estimate an average yield of 16 kg per hectare. According to agricultural extension agents in the province of Albacete, Spain, the productions per hectare were reported as 6 kg in the first year, 12 kg in the second year, and 10 kg in the third year.

In the region of Sardinia, Italy, floral production per hectare is estimated to be around 650,000-700,000 flowers (equivalent to 5 kg of dried stigmas) in the first year, about 1,300,000-1,400,000 flowers (10 kg of dried stigmas) in the second year, and 1,950,000-2,100,000 flowers (15 kg of dried stigmas) in the third year. In the fourth year, production returns to around 1,300,000-1,400,000 flowers (10 kg of dried stigmas).

To obtain 1 kilogram of dried stigmas, approximately 140,000 flowers need to be harvested, equivalent to 75 kg in fresh weight.

The estimated production per hectare can be summarized as follows:

- Number of flowers produced: 1,400,000

- Weight of flowers produced: 750 kg

- Fresh stigmas produced: 50 kg

- Dried stigmas produced: 10 kg

The yield of "crude" saffron, i.e., fresh stigmas, is 5 kg for every 75 kg of harvested flowers. With drying, the fresh stigmas lose approximately 4/5 of their weight, so 5 kg of fresh stigmas result in 1 kg of dried stigmas.

In addition to the stigmas, other parts of the plant are used for secondary products. The leaves and bulb-tubers can be utilized as feed for livestock, especially sheep and cows, as they contribute to increased and improved milk secretion.

Separation of stigmas

The phase of saffron flower harvesting is followed by the so-called "trimming" or "deflowering" (known as "monda de la rosa" in Spain). This operation is carried out manually and involves cutting the flower below the point of separation of the three stigmas, avoiding as much as possible the inclusion of the yellowish style, which could devalue the product. This is a straightforward activity but requires experience, especially to identify the optimal point for separating the style from the stigmas.

The "deflowering" must be completed on the same day as the flower harvest to prevent the stigmas from wilting, and it is usually performed on worktables. Until now, this operation has been done solely manually, but recently, in Macedonia, a semi-automatic machine has been developed that separates the stigmas and stamens, whose weight is higher than that of the petals, using an air current generated by a fan. However, the manual process is still used when aiming to obtain a high-quality product.

On average, 1 kg of flowers produces approximately 72 g of fresh stigmas, which correspond to 12 g of dried saffron. Therefore, it may take up to 200,000 flowers to produce 1 kg of saffron. This manual and labor-intensive process is one of the reasons why saffron is considered the most expensive spice in the world.

In Sardinia, instead, only the manual method is used, which involves cutting the flower at the tube of the perianth, without opening the petals with the fingernail or using a pair of scissors, and only later separating the stigmas from the rest of the flower, which is discarded. An experienced trimmer can work on 600-700 flowers per hour, resulting in approximately 4g of dried product.

Drying of the Stigmas

The dehydration phase is an essential post-harvest treatment to transform the saffron stigmas into the spice we know. During this process, the stigmas experience a loss of about 80% of their original weight. The color, flavor, and overall quality of saffron depend on the drying method used, as it involves the hydrolysis of crocin and related pigments. The chemical changes that occur in the stigmas during drying influence the taste and potency of the final spice. High-quality saffron has a pleasant, floral, and delicately spicy flavor with a slightly bitter note. A low moisture content, preferably below 12% as defined by the ISO3632 standard, helps maintain the product's quality for a longer period. Additionally, the saffron's moisture during storage also affects the color quality.

The drying process can vary from country to country, with two main methods in terms of temperature. In some countries like India, Morocco, and Iran, the saffron stigmas are dried at room temperature, directly exposed to sunlight or in well-ventilated environments. In India, the stigmas are sun-dried for 3-5 days until their moisture content is reduced to 8-10%, resulting in the highest quality saffron. The remaining parts of the flower are also sun-dried for 3-5 days, lightly beaten with sticks, and then immersed in water. The parts that float are discarded, while those that sink are collected and further dried, becoming the second-grade saffron. The discarded parts of the flower, treated as described above, constitute the third-grade saffron.

In Morocco, the saffron stigmas are spread out on a cloth

in a very thin layer and dried in the sun for several hours or in the shade for 7-10 days. This is a low-temperature drying process. On the other hand, in Spain, Greece, and Italy, a second method of high-temperature drying is used, where the stigmas are exposed to hot air or a heat source.

In the Navelli Plateau, Italy, the saffron stigmas are placed in a well-spread sieve positioned above a live fire of oakwood at about 20 cm distance. The sieve is suspended by three cords so that it can be easily rotated, ensuring even drying. During the process, the stigmas are turned to ensure uniform drying on both sides. The toasting process lasts between 15 to 20 minutes. Dehydration is considered complete when the stigmas, pressed between the fingers, do not break and retain some elasticity. This traditional toasting method over a live fire preserves the deep red color, fragrance, and aroma of saffron. Tests carried out with electric dryers have confirmed that stigmas dried over a live fire using the traditional method retain better organoleptic qualities.

During the toasting process, the stigmas lose approximately 4/5 of their weight. For example, from 500g of fresh stigmas, 100g of dried stigmas are obtained. The final product maintains a moisture content between 5% and 20%. The dried stigmas can be subsequently ground into powder using an electric coffee grinder, ready for use as a spice.

In Spain, during the drying process, it is common to place a second sieve over the first one to flip the stigmas without directly handling them, thus avoiding fragmentation. This method ensures better results in preserving the integrity of the product. Drying in Spain is done on wood stoves, braziers, or rustic fireplaces, but the heat source is always wood.

In Greece, several drying methods are used: shadow drying for about 5-10 days, spreading the filaments on the ground or on nets; sun drying for 3-4 days, leaving the saffron exposed to the open air; drying in a wood-fired oven for about 10 minutes.

In Sardegna, before the drying process, they practice a method called "feidadura," which involves lightly impregnating the stigmas with extra virgin olive oil. The amount of oil used is about one-quarter of a coffee spoon for 100g of fresh saffron. Through this operation, they believe that the appearance of saffron is improved, and its shelf life is extended.

Furthermore, it should be noted that drying represents a crucial process, as it is during this phase that the hydrolysis of crocin and related pigments occurs. The chemical changes in the stigmas during drying influence the flavor and strength of the final spice, making care and precision during the drying phase essential to obtain high-quality saffron.

All producers agree that it is ideal to carry out the separation of stigmas on the same day as the harvest. When this is not possible, the flowers are placed on plastic sheets, spread on the floor in well-ventilated areas, in layers no thicker than 10 cm, to prevent them from sticking together or the stigmas from being damaged under excessive weight. The optimal point of drying is around 10% residual humidity to avoid the packaging process being too delicate.

The drying method can influence the size and volume of the final product. Higher temperatures and longer drying times can lead to a shortening of the length and reduced volume of saffron.

Studies have been conducted on different drying methods, and it has been observed that traditional sun drying performed in India requires a period of time between 27 and 53 hours, which could cause enzymatic degradation of crocin, the main pigment in saffron. A shorter drying method and controlled temperature can produce higher-quality saffron.

Research has compared various drying methods, including shade drying, open-air drying, sun drying, electric ovens, cross-flow drying, vacuum drying, and dehumidified drying. Some of these studies have indicated that drying at controlled temperatures, such as $40 \pm 5°C$ (solar dryer or oven dryer), is the best way to maintain high saffron quality while saving time compared to traditional sun drying. Other studies compared traditional drying, a Spanish variant at 55°C, and microwave drying (300 watts), and found that microwave-dried saffron had better color retention, aroma, and bitter taste.

In general, the drying process is crucial to maintain the quality and characteristics of saffron, and it is carried out with care and precision to achieve a high-quality final product.

Moisture control

It is essential to control the average moisture level of the product before packaging. If the percentage of moisture becomes excessive, it may exceed the limits imposed by regulations or fail to meet the requirements of a potential buyer. Furthermore, high humidity can promote the growth of molds and yeasts and cause the loss of the coloring power due to the dissolution of crocins, the main pigments of saffron. Moisture values can vary between saffron in filaments and saffron in powder, with the former typically having higher moisture content.

In Sardinia, moisture checks are rarely performed as analysis results have confirmed that the moisture content of the product never exceeds 10%.

In Western Macedonia, saffron is accepted by the "saffron cooperative" only if the moisture does not exceed 11.5%. If the moisture exceeds this value, the product undergoes further drying in specific ovens to achieve the desired moisture level before being packaged and sold.

Quality

After complete drying, saffron must be immediately stored in perfectly covered or sealed containers and protected from light to avoid bleaching. The final product consists of thin threads, ranging in color from dark orange to reddish-brown, approximately 1 inch in length. True saffron has a pleasantly spicy, pungent, and bitter taste, with a lingering aroma. It is available both in threads and in powder form, but long and dark red threads are generally preferred over powder, as the latter can be easily adulterated.

The quality of saffron depends on its color (concentration of crocin), taste (picrocrocin), and aroma (safranal). The best quality saffron has a high crocin absorption capacity (> 190) at 440 nm, a picrocrocin absorption capacity (25-30) at 330 nm, and a safranal absorption capacity (100) at a wavelength of 257 nm.

Fresh saffron appears glossy and greasy to the touch, but over time, it becomes dull and brittle. Storage in the dark and in environments with low temperature and relative humidity is important to preserve its quality. Due to its high price, saffron is often subjected to adulteration. To increase its weight, water is frequently added, or in some cases, petroleum or glycerin is used to improve its appearance. Sometimes, flowers from other plants, such as Carthamus tinctorius, Calendula officinalis, or Arnica, are fraudulently added to genuine saffron stigmas.

Production, harvest and bulb preservation

In plants with a multi-year cycle, leaf emergence begins in the autumn, about two weeks earlier than in plants with an annual cycle. The greatest length development of the leaf apparatus is observed in the months of March-April when the leaves can reach up to 40 cm in length. Already in the month of May, a progressive wilting of the leaves can be noticed. During the period of March-April, the vegetative activity allows the accumulation of reserve materials in the new bulb-tubers, formed from the bulb-tuber that bloomed the previous year, promoting their enlargement. This process ceases as summer approaches when the plants enter dormancy and lose their leaves and roots completely.

The production of bulb-tubers is variable in terms of quantity and number. A single bulb-tuber can produce up to 10-11, but on average, it is around 3-4 bulb-tubers. It is important to note that less productive bulb-tubers provide material capable of producing flowers in the same year of planting or resuming the production cycle. The formation of new bulb-tubers occurs above the ones planted previously, which gradually decrease in size and flatten. With reproduction, the new bulb-tubers gradually rise to the surface of the ground, overlapping the production of the previous year.

This reproductive process justifies, in the multi-year cultivation, the adoption of a greater planting depth compared to the annual cultivation (about double). Additionally, after several years, it is necessary to carry out the removal of bulb-tubers because when they are brought too close to the surface, their productivity decreases. This is an important aspect to consider for maintaining sustainable production in the long term.

The removal of saffron bulb-tubers is carried out when the foliage of the plants has dried up. In Italy, it is customary to perform the removal in the month of July, while in Spain, it is preferred to do it in May or early June. This difference in timing is due to the fact that in Spain, the soil is less hard during that period, making the removal process easier. Additionally, there is more time for selecting the bulb-tubers to be replanted for new production cycles, which are anticipated compared to the planting time in Italy.

Traditionally, bulb-tuber removal was done solely by hand, using a hoe to uncover the bulb-tubers, which were then hand-collected and placed in baskets. However, with the advancement of agricultural technologies, small plows pulled by tractors are now used to create deep furrows, approximately 20 cm deep, to uncover the bulb-tubers. These are then collected and stored in baskets or hemp sacks.

Recently, the effectiveness of an adapted potato digger for saffron bulb-tubers has been tested by the Institute of Agricultural Mechanics at the University of Florence. This new approach has shown economically and technically valid results, especially in looser and less compact soils. These new solutions can facilitate the bulb-tuber removal process and improve the efficiency of cultivating the precious saffron.

The preservation of saffron bulbs after harvesting is an important aspect to avoid premature sprouting and to optimize flowering. Various studies have demonstrated that temperature and relative humidity significantly influence the bulb preservation process.

Koltsova reported that bulbs harvested in May and stored in boxes covered with soil at a temperature of 19-23°C and a relative humidity of 65-75% sprout and bloom much earlier compared to those stored at 23-27°C or left in the ground.

Benschop indicated that Crocus bulbs can be stored at a temperature of 25°C and a relative humidity of 80% for up to 8 months, thus delaying flowering. Similarly, Munoz-Gomez and others stated that storing bulbs at a temperature of 30°C for 45 days increased the number of flowers, but the result was a very low number of flowers per bulb.

Molina and others reported that storing bulbs at 25°C for more than 5 months causes the death of the flower bud. They also observed that seeds can be stored at 25°C for 90-115 days.

Further research has shown that bulbs harvested after leaf withering and stored at 2°C in an environment with 1% oxygen for 70 days can be forced to flower from early December to the end of January, achieving the same saffron yield as bulbs stored at normal temperatures in Spain. However, storage at freezing temperatures (0 or -1°C) can damage the bulbs.

In summary, the temperature and relative humidity during

the storage of saffron bulbs can be adjusted based on the flowering and saffron production scheduling needs, but care must be taken to avoid damaging the bulbs with extreme temperatures.

And finally, the sale.

As mentioned at the beginning, we are not convinced that agriculture is meant to become a source of money. This only triggers the classic capitalist dynamics that have proven to be anything but beneficial and sustainable, creating a vicious circle.

However, since we promised assistance with the sale in the title, here are three possible points to consider:

Word of mouth among friends and acquaintances, a fairly straightforward choice, although you may not be able to sell a large quantity of spice... unless you are a highly skilled local influencer. It's a good start, nonetheless.

Participating in local markets for regional products is a good option. They are often beautiful and characteristic, but it does require a small investment in a gazebo, various equipment, customized packaging, and a more substantial investment in time to obtain the necessary permits and participate in markets near or far from home on weekends. Nonetheless, it's worth trying, especially since transporting saffron doesn't require large vehicles; you can even use a bicycle, which would make your presence more credible and impressive.

Selling online through a personal website, social media, and various marketplace platforms is another option. However, it opens up a world of opportunities, but unless you have abundant production, it may not be cost-effective due to the high costs involved in investments, time, and effort required to obtain all the necessary permits, organize product shipments, including agreements with express couriers and suitable packaging, and manage all the related issues such as refunds, returns, and unexpected challenges.

Finally, another option is to look for a wholesaler and sell the entire batch at once. This may lower the price, but it's up to you to decide. You could opt for a quick sale with fewer profits or the possibility of slowly building a solid and loyal local customer base.

Good luck!!!